The Bee Story

TEACHINGS ON PATRUL RINPOCHE'S

The Drama of the Flower-Gathering Garden

Dza Patrul Rinpoche (1808-1887)
Courtesy of Shechen Monastery

The Bee Story

TEACHINGS ON PATRUL RINPOCHE'S

The Drama of the Flower-Gathering Garden

Dzigar Kongtrul Rinpoche

ORIGINAL ILLUSTRATIONS BY
Tara Di Gesu

ROAR OF THE
FEARLESS LION

*With this publication of The Bee Story, we are pleased to introduce the Roar of
the Fearless Lion, an imprint for the published teachings of Dzigar Kongtrul
Rinpoche. Publications in print and digital as well as audio and video recordings
fall within the scope of this imprint.*

May Patrul Rinpoche's beloved Dharma tale continue to inspire countless practitioners to renounce their false assumptions about samsara and impress in their minds the irrefutable lessons of impermanence.

May the noble Longchen Nyingtik lineage flower continuously in our world throughout the present age and beyond.

Table of Contents

Editors' Preface

Part I of these teachings from Venerable Dzigar Kongtrul Rinpoche has been edited from the transcribed text of four public talks given in May 1998 as a sequence of "Personal Link" presentations. In three of these talks, Rinpoche reads from the English text translated by Tulku Thondup, found in *Enlightened Living, Teachings of Tibetan Buddhist Masters; Chapter 2, Holy Dharma Advice, A Drama in the Lotus Garden,* by Patrul Rinpoche (Shambhala, Boston, MA 1990). Used here with permission.

In one of those public talks, Kongtrul Rinpoche reads from a portion of his own translation of this text from the Tibetan that he made with Elizabeth Mattis Namgyel, titled *The Drama of the Flower-Gathering Garden.*

Part II contains the entirety of Rinpoche's original translation, affectionately referred to as *The Bee Story,* along with his 1990 commentary on that translation. Though we do not have an audio record, the translation and commentary were thoughtfully preserved by Mary, one of Rinpoche's earliest students, from San Pablo, California.

We apologize to Rinpoche and to the lineage for any errors or misrepresentations, for which we take full responsibility.

Introduction by Dzigar Kongtrul Rinpoche

The Dharma King Chöjé Patrul Rinpoche's poetic and creative story of Golden Bee and Turquoise Bee gives us great insight into the downfalls of life's preoccupations. We spend almost all our time absorbed in acquiring and attending to countless pursuits—wealth and status, beauty and our physique, love, relationships, family, etc. In time, due to changing circumstances and the nature of impermanence, each one of these pursuits eventually fails us, and in turn brings us great grief and pain. When this eventuality occurs, people are generally lost in hopelessness and a state of despair. In trying to soothe themselves while in such states of bewilderment and pain, they can often make wrong choices. They cling to shadows of the past and repeatedly attempt to recreate whatever it is that they have lost, only to lose it all again and again. *The Bee Story* is so deeply inspiring because Wide Wings was able to use the pain of his life falling apart to help wake himself up; he was able to transfer or expand the love and commitment he had for his beloved to the path of awakening. Ultimately, this not only allowed him to resolve his short-term suffering, but it also opened the door for him to pursue freedom for himself and his beloved, escaping the delusion of samsara altogether.

This particular set of teachings—which, thanks to the efforts of Suzy Greanias, Mark Kram, Radha Marcum, Chris Parmentier, Andrew Shakespeare, Markus Stobbs, and Joey Waxman has now become the book you hold in your hand— was my first attempt to teach to a Western audience. The story is captivating, and the imagery and poetry are moving. Patrul Rinpoche uses these aspects as a vehicle to present teachings on the profound meaning of Dharma, particularly in the face of life's tragedies, and in the end, he shows us the triumph and resilience of our awakened mind. I welcome all who read this book to first take a deep, wholesome sigh, and then, as the story unfolds, turn inward to look squarely at one's own enmeshments. We have so many pursuits which will be affected, sooner or later, by the inevitable changes in circumstances and the impermanence of our lives and the world. May this little story be an inspiration to live simply, turning away from all the various ways we tend to complicate our lives and our world. May it show us how to be profoundly in the present moment, and to pursue a greater purpose and meaning through the practice of Dharma, just as the main character, Wide Wings, does in the story.

—Dzigar Kongtrul Rinpoche

Part I:

Translation by Tulku Thondup
with 1998 Commentary by
Dzigar Kongtrul Rinpoche

Part I: Overview

This beloved story, written in Tibetan by Patrul Rinpoche, is based on the true story of a prominent couple from Derge in Eastern Tibet. The man in the story would go on to become one of the most important siddhas in the Derge kingdom and was also the general secretary of the Derge king. His wife was a beautiful woman from an esteemed Tibetan family and was admired throughout the country as a great lady. Their tragic story unfolds as they are compelled to separate in life, first through disease and quarantine, and then in death. The story relates what the couple went through together and what happened to the one who was left behind.

Personally, I've enjoyed this story from a young age and always felt a tremendous connection with it. It's an important teaching story in Tibet, written by a preeminent master in our lineage. Not only do I appreciate its poetry, but I am deeply moved by the truths conveyed regarding the things of this world. So, I thought it would be useful for students to read this—not because I wish to suggest a particular response but rather to simply expose people to this well-loved Tibetan Buddhist story. Writing it as a poetic drama, Patrul Rinpoche begins by paying homage to Manjushri, his wisdom deity. In the translation by Tulku Thondup, the title is *Holy Dharma Advice: A Drama in the Lotus Garden*. Elizabeth and I made a translation of this a long time ago, but we called it *The Bee Story*.

The point of reading this dharmic story is to reflect on it and resist the naiveté that one naturally experiences in adopting the view of permanence—pretending there is plenty of time to do all the things you want to do—meanwhile only getting around to practicing Dharma near the end. It may be true that you do actually have a lot of time left. However, recently I spoke with someone who mentioned that she'd led a very full life, and though it may look to others like her life had been long and full, in the end, it seemed very short to her. She said, "Life goes by so fast, in the blink of an eye." On the one hand, she felt she'd lived a long life; on the other, in her mind and in her experience, it had all gone by so quickly. Then she told me that until she met the Dharma, she felt there hadn't been much point to life. The Dharma gave meaning to her life. It could be that many students reading or listening right now are young, bright, and intelligent. You may think you have a long life ahead of you. You might live into your eighties, nineties, or even to a hundred years old. But when you actually reach that age—just like my friend who was personally devoted to the Dharma and who lived very fully—it still seems that it's over in the blink of an eye.

Or it could be that some of us will die very soon. There may be certain questions in your mind. Am I really healthy? Should I consult a doctor? Am I ready to find out that I'm not well or that I have a terminal illness? Is it better to avoid finding out, or is it better to know? If we do find out—say, for instance, that I have throat cancer or lung cancer or bone marrow cancer—what will it be like to hear that? What will I do when I find out? There is resistance to knowing and fully accepting the fact that we may be sick even at this very minute. Even though we may recognize in our unconscious mind that one day we are going to die, we have a tremendous resistance to acknowledging that and fully accepting it.

When we read stories like this one, with unconscious fears in the back of our minds, every reading brings those fears to the surface. That's the point of reading this story. Yet there isn't much purpose if we cannot then turn our minds toward the Dharma, toward death, and learn to let go, to accept impermanence and death as a part of our lives, surrendering ourselves fully to the Three Jewels. Otherwise, what's the point?

People come to me when their parents are terminally ill. They tell me that it's really hard to talk to their parents when they are unable to accept their condition. They ask whether it's important for their parents to know they're dying, or if they should pretend everything is okay and just let them die. My view is this: If someone has a tremendous resistance to knowing they're dying because they don't know what to do with that information, and it's already too late to do anything about it, then maybe it is better not to confront that person—better for them not to know. My sense is that when somebody is very sick, how could they *not* know they're dying? Many times, they do actually know yet are still not ready to face it. They're not ready to let go or to give up hope. In that case, what's the point of telling them they're going to die or that they have a very short time left to live?

If this person is a practitioner, then it's a different case. It is important to know when you're dying, so you can better prepare for it. Having worked with many dying people, I've noticed that even practitioners don't find it easy to hear that they're dying. They don't easily give up their hopes or let go of their attachments to this life until the last minute. When somebody is a practitioner, I think even then the level of faith in the Three Jewels or in the scriptures is still not certain. Though one has taken refuge and become a practitioner, one's faith—a sense of total trust and surrender of one's life to the Three Jewels—may not necessarily be strong. Even in the case of lamas, the lama himself may be ready, but the disciples may not be ready. They want to take the lama out to eat or to rest at some great hospital to consult with doctors who counsel their patients about amazing surgeries. The disciples don't recognize what they're doing, or perhaps their neuroses will not let them hear it, so they hold onto their attachments and hopes. Many lamas nowadays, as you know, die in hospitals. Perhaps it doesn't matter to a lama so much because the lama is very accomplished, but this portrays very clearly the hopes and attachments of the people around the lama.

If you can, confront your fears of imminent death in this life, and prior to that, your fear of sickness. Even prior to sickness, confront your old age—although you may not feel old yet—and overcome your greatest fears. Don't allow those fears to remain in your unconscious mind while living continually in denial, with the pretense that there is any permanence in this world. Instead, if we show great courage, it will simplify our life.

That becomes very clear in something Jetsun Mila once said. Somebody told him that he must be Maitreya, the reincarnation of a great, enlightened being, because when that person contemplated Mila's life, it was amazing to recognize what he'd done—from beginning to end. He simply could not be an ordinary person. In response, Jetsun Mila said, "It's good to think in that way from the dharmic point of view, from the point of view of increasing your devotion. But from another side of the dharmic view, if I have truly become wise now, then it's a great insult to the Dharma and to me, because it's as if the Dharma hadn't really changed me very much, or that I hadn't accomplished much through the Dharma." He said, "If people had the relentless feeling of remorse for their deeds, a fear of the lower realms, and a strong sense of imminent death, like a piercing thorn in their heart, they would accomplish something similar to what I have accomplished. People would assert themselves on the path as I have asserted myself on the path."

So, if we truly realize that we are here on this earth like guests from another world, staying only a few days—that life spent on this earth is a gift today and every day—then the stress produced by all of the hopes, fears, and situations in which we try to secure our life would be greatly reduced. This is true not only in our own life, but in our family members' lives, too, with their long-term plans, strategies, hopes, and fears. When you go on vacation, you don't put a lot of time, effort, or energy into fixing up the hotel room as if you're going to live there a long time. You focus more on enjoyment, on taking advantage of your retreat and the resort. Just like that, if you realize your situation and act accordingly, even if it is just for a few days, you won't be bothered by all of the long-term plans and strategies, hopes, fears, and stress. Instead, you'll be able to enjoy your life as it is.

No one here today is terribly sick at this point, and everyone has enough money to live on or has the ability to earn a living. Just recently there were so many job opportunities in America that it was difficult to find enough people to take all the available positions. Many restaurants had special offers, and they even went into high schools to recruit people. Even if you live in an unusual situation, like a sangha house, you still have enough money to buy decent clothes. But consider what Shantideva and the teachings suggest—"Don't treat this body too lavishly; it will never be completely satisfied. Make sure that you put this body to work, as it should be put to work. Have some food and some clothes, have a shelter to accommodate this body, but make sure you don't lavishly cherish this body. Put this body to work because if you lavishly cherish it, this body will become the source of all your attachments, the source of all your pain."

From that point of view, life is very straightforward and simple. We can truly contemplate the impermanence of this life and our imminent death that approaches year by year, month by month, day by day. As hard as it is to face death, why create more attachments? You can't get rid of attachments unless you give up the hope of cherishing this life and this body. Each hope is an attachment in itself. There are a lot of struggles to work through. Once you accomplish something, it leads to further attachments. Life may feel very hard because you have to go through birth, old age, sickness, and death, as well as face unfavorable circumstances and depart from favorable ones. On top of that, we make it much more difficult for ourselves. However, life can be made very simple by contemplating impermanence and imminent death.

Dharma provides simplicity whether you admit it or not. You have a body that is capable of creating samsara, but if you use it to accomplish Dharma, this human body is also remarkably capable. The human body is said to be the greatest

15

of all physical bodies, the most supreme body. In the god realms, beings have bodies of light. Because of their light bodies, they can take advantage of what that kind of body can achieve—having a tremendously long life with all of the medical powers that we could ever imagine. On the other hand, a light body is not supreme for practicing the Vajrayana path or cultivating the enlightened mind.

In the lower realms we see animal bodies. They may be beautiful to look at, but we see how much change, suffering, and threat they experience all the time. They lack wisdom and intelligence even though they may have great instincts. Most people won't even consider how much suffering there is in the hungry ghost and the hell realms. This human body is a very special gift, given to each of us through our own good merit and good fortune.

The time we live in is different from any other because there have been buddhas and bodhisattvas who have taught the Dharma, particularly the Vajrayana Dharma. If you are motivated, you can put this body of yours toward the work of discovering the enlightened nature we all have. That potential is present not just in the mind but also in physical attributes of our bodies.

Of course, food sustains our bodies during life. *The Words of My Perfect Teacher* states that if a famine were to occur in the world and grain were weighed against gold, the disciples of the Buddha would never starve to death, though they may struggle along with everyone else. One of the great teachers of the Longchen Nyingtik once had hardly anything to eat while he was receiving a teaching. Because his body was so weak, he fell down twice on his way to fetch water. His teacher, watching from a window, saw him fall. The teacher said, "When I see him suffer this way, I can't help but feel that I should give him some food. I feel I should help him. But I know what he's doing is for his own benefit. What he's going through is a purification, so I don't want to disrupt that." I doubt whether any of us have gone through something like that or will have to go through that. Jetsun Mila is another good example of someone who went through great hardship and purification through the body.

In some sense, once you've taken refuge in the Three Jewels from the bottom of your heart—really giving up cherishing and protecting this life and making the best use of it to accomplish Dharma—then much of the work is already done. You already have a body. You will have the food you require. Even if there comes a time when grains of rice and barley are weighed against gold and diamonds, a disciple will never starve. When you can trust that, then food is taken care of. As for clothes, you'll always have something to wear, and even if you had nothing to wear, what's so bad about being naked? As for a place to live, there is always somewhere to shelter yourself.

In our retreat cabins, I stay in one place. That may not be so great because as Jigme Lingpa said, "The sun and moon are adored by every single being because of their good qualities, but imagine if the sun and moon stayed in one place!" Everyone would hate it. So, when you stay in one place, there's always a danger of cultivating attachments to loved ones, family, friends, and relatives, as well as hateful beings—people with whom you have conflict. That's just the way it is, even if you're as perfect as the Buddha himself. His cousin, Devadatta, who served the Buddha for twenty-five years, still went against him and walked away with many negative feelings. You can't avoid yourself. Even if you're perfect, you still have to deal with the projections of other people. So maybe there's not really anything so great about having a home or staying in one place for too long. If you want to travel, you can always find a place to live, a place to shelter yourself from time to time.

It's interesting that when certain people hear teachings like this, they feel something arising in them from deep down. They feel very inspired and connected. For others, that doesn't happen. Chandrakirti said that we can tell who has a connection to the emptiness teachings because, for those who do, just hearing the word *emptiness* causes a tingle to rise up from within. They

17

are completely moved. Tears run from their eyes, and they feel a tremendous joy and satisfaction found nowhere else. They intuitively recognize a connection to the emptiness teachings and know that they'll be benefited by them.

As we know from *The Words of My Perfect Teacher*, there are others who don't feel a similar attraction. When Atisha gave teachings on emptiness and egolessness of the self, two shravakas who came to hear him enjoyed and appreciated his teachings tremendously. But when Atisha gave teachings on the egolessness of the dharma, they covered their ears and cried, "Please, don't say these things!"

For those who have this connection, something truly clicks in them—even if their toes don't tingle and their heart isn't so moved that tears fall from their eyes. For others, it's almost abhorrent to hear such teachings. One is not necessarily bad or the other good. However, one's life can become more refined by reflecting on one's experience of the teachings in this way.

Nothing can be done to change the karma of beings. If it were possible, the buddhas and bodhisattvas would have done that a long time ago. When I read Patrul Rinpoche's teachings and contemplate his lifestyle, I appreciate them. But I don't expect everyone to have the same response to Patrul Rinpoche's teachings that I have. We have a saying in Tibetan, "Renunciation is like a fuzzy dandelion. From a distance, the seed head can appear very thick and furry, but when you blow on it just slightly, it goes *poof*! It all flies up into the air."

Think about your individual self—the good qualities as well as the bad—the loneliness, the sense of immensely saddened mind, depression, or hopelessness. From far off, some of us who have that "furry" kind of renunciation may fantasize about being a yogi and living a simple renunciate's life, but when it comes to truly facing what's necessary, it may prove extremely difficult. So, in that sense, it's hard to trust what others say—or even yourself, for that matter.

When Trungpa Rinpoche passed away, one monk praised Trungpa Rinpoche's activities and also praised many of the students. He spoke about Trungpa Rinpoche's great achievements and where the students could go. Then at the end of his remarks, he repeated a very famous saying in Tibetan, "Until that time when your skull hits the ground, you never know what kind of practitioner you will be." At that point, if you have accomplished something meaningful, then you have accomplished it. If you haven't accomplished anything, then no matter how much glory or fame you might have achieved in this world as a so-called "great practitioner," you'll most likely end up in the lower realms.

It's much different if someone actually does have genuine feelings of renunciation. This morning I was talking with one of my senior students. Most of the time he totally bullshits me, but today I could tell he was sincere in saying he had a real glimpse of the suffering and the pointlessness of pursuing the activities of this life. I doubt whether he's going to renounce anything right away or even do anything different from what he has been doing in his life. But having that glimpse has probably given him much more freedom in his mind. For that moment, he could see how to live his life more in accordance with the Dharma and perhaps let go of the struggle, the hopes and fears around this life.

Maybe other students also have had such glimpses. Whether anything comes out of that or not, it leaves what we call in the Dharma "an impression on your alaya," so that maybe in our future lives this will become strong enough for something truly meaningful to arise from it. On one hand, temporal renunciation is not anything great; on the other hand, temporal renunciation and a saddening mind—seeing the pointlessness of this life and all that we pursue—implies that our future lives may go fully toward the Dharma. So, it's important to appreciate that and not to disregard it.

It's a matter of distinguishing that particular taste, a matter of your ambition, and of seeking a different kind of enjoyment in how you make this life serve you. From a very realistic and practical point of view, living a simple life and pursuing the

Dharma as much as you can will totally protect you from a complicated life. If you can embrace the experience of sadness, depression, or the loneliness of retreat with the greatest depth of melancholy and without rejecting these experiences through aversion, they can be very powerful forces—stirring deep reflection and serving as the source of tremendous peace. You just let go of your struggles and experience their rawness, along with a sense of vision. You won't find this anywhere else, especially if you are distracted by life's attractions.

There is a saying, "When Mila looks at sentient beings, sentient beings appear crazy. When sentient beings look at Mila, Mila appears crazy." Despite such differences in perception, it's clear that the amount of suffering Mila endured in his pursuit of Dharma—all the hardships from the time he was with Marpa to his time in the mountains by himself, eating nettles for years—was worth it in the end. It all paid off greatly and transformed a sentient being into an enlightened being.

Whatever we try so hard to be—the struggle and pain we go through to achieve "success" or glory in this life—of what purpose is it in the end? We must leave it all anyway to go beyond. Even at the peak of President Clinton's presidency— the most glorious time of his life and what he'd worked for so hard—we can see how many complications and how much pain and suffering he experienced. Seeing that, we can understand very well how those who are not in such prominent positions suffer even more.

From a dharmic point of view, when you contemplate what it is that you strive to achieve as the central purpose of your life—with all the struggle that you go through to attain it—you can see it just complicates your life. In the end, it causes you to endure even more pain and suffering. There's not really any decent payback or payoff. Whether you believe the Dharma or you completely disregard it, that is still the dharmic point of view. Before you reject it completely, I think it would be worthwhile—especially since everyone here today has taken refuge—to at least consider how much truth there is in that view. Is there a pointlessness and suffering that is the main feature of the world, in others' lives, and in your life? If the Dharma should prove to be wrong and your doubts prove to be right, then I assure you the Dharma won't be offended. The Dharma is present expressly for guiding and protecting you from complications, struggles, and suffering.

If the Dharma proves to be *right*, then perhaps you need to contemplate the point of your struggles. What is the point of all the suffering and struggling you've spent time on in the past, or that you are spending time on now and plan to spend time on in the future? Look closely into the Dharma. See what the Dharma really suggests. When you look at it closely, you may find that your interests become a little different after thorough examination. Perhaps your interests will become more genuine when you have a sincere wish to find some resolution and salvation from pain and suffering. You may even find it very *practical*, though so often we think the Dharma and these suggestions to be *impractical*. I know that I am an impractical person at times—so *I* may prove to be impractical—but the Dharma is not. The Dharma offers concrete suggestions, solutions, and methods, along with the wisdom of which steps to take and precisely how to take those steps.

I may not be capable of presenting this to you very clearly and exactly, but if you look into the Dharma, you will find it is very clear. My mistakes will all be cleared away. At some point, your relationship with the dharmic viewpoint will likely involve a struggle because any change, any transition involves struggle. Of course, at the beginning, anything that helps you to turn away from where you are heading can be difficult. It's very natural for there to be a difficult struggle in the beginning of any venture or activity. But as you slowly adjust to the ideas and the ways of the Dharma and take those steps, slowly and gradually making improvements—mostly on the inside, in your mind—then at some point you will think about your accomplishments in the Dharma, about what you have attained, and feel good about yourself. You will feel quite happy about yourself and what you're doing. That is also very inspiring for the future—to have a life that is simple, uncomplicated, straightforward, and easy, with few struggles and much delight.

Then you can do exactly as Patrul Rinpoche, Jamyang Khyentse Wangpo, Jamgon Kongtrul Lodro Thaye, or any of the lineage gurus have done—to think only of making what little progress you can in this lifetime. It becomes very simple when your mind is all that is required, along with adopting a direction of honest sincerity and some basic methods to avoid obstacles, such as prayers, supplications, and taking refuge.

When you think about how you usually strive in the conventional world, with endless talk and work, then of course you may no longer feel interested in it. But let's say for now that you *are* interested—you're inspired to *do* something. That requires more than just your mind alone. It requires resources and personal skills, which don't just happen by themselves. You need training; you have to go to school or receive instruction, and you need to spend a lot of time and energy. Even after you have all of that, you'll also need to have the interpersonal and communication skills to relate well to others and work productively with them. Those skills don't come naturally to some people. They may have good public relations skills like patience, tolerance, and understanding, but these may not yield much of a return for them. Others might be really patient but still have to work alone because they can't take working with other people all the time.

Unquestionably, there's a lot that is positive to be found in struggle, but so many aspects of life can lead to a negative outcome. Some personal disasters may end not just in defeat for yourself, but also in your inflicting pain on others or their inflicting pain on you. Additionally, there is the "law of the land" to consider. Sometimes it's another person who turns you over to the law, and the law determines a judgment. Even when no one intends for anything negative to happen in the beginning, unforeseen circumstances and momentum may lead from one problem to the next. In this way, tremendous problems occur—country versus country, political group versus political group, family versus family, parents versus parents, children versus parents, and friend versus friend.

We see in the news and on TV the consequences of wrongdoing being judged and punished. Even someone who wins a legal battle or an election may temporarily feel good, but in the end, nothing truly beneficial comes from it because of all of the negative karma generated by having inflicted pain on others. The so-called *winners* then have to suffer the effects of that karma. Whether worldly law or consensus is on your side or not, if you inflict pain on others by bringing conventional law against someone who inflicted pain on you, this is merely the law of the land or society. It doesn't resolve your karma; it perpetuates it.

What resolves your karma with others and yourself? One has to *experience* that karma. For example, those who work to put someone into the electric chair—whatever it is that the person may have done wrong—may think they've won a victory. But in the end, they are responsible for putting that person into the electric chair and will have to face that karma. The convicted person goes to the electric chair, but maybe those who put that person there will have to go to another "chair" that's even worse. In the electric chair, you only die once. In the case of the hell realms, in the first hell, the Reviving Hell, you die every second, revive, and then die again. That is considered to be the hell of all hells because you actually die, whereas in most of the hell realms, you don't die. So, you have no break. The Reviving Hell is among the eight other hells. There is that kind of pain and suffering, and you have to watch it all happening to you.

Struggling in the world and in life—in all we are trying to do—is not like going to war. We're not talking about that kind of situation. We're just talking about facing the chaos and problems of conventional life. Even if it doesn't happen to the extent I've mentioned, every couple in the sangha quarrels at least once a month. Husbands say something; wives react. Your lover says something and you react. At other times, you really dissolve into each other's eyes, particularly when you're making love. But when you're in a quarrel or when you're fighting, just the sight of the other person totally revolts you and causes you tremendous pain. Harsh words and all of the unintentional games that go on in a relationship for one to gain a victory over the other create an absolutely horrible feeling, a horrible experience. It's only natural, as we say, for couples to quarrel, but that doesn't justify the pain.

Nonetheless, the pain and suffering don't go away. Of course, people can make up in the end; otherwise, they split up. But the pain and suffering stores up like money in the bank. You put one dollar, two dollars, three dollars into the bank, and at some point, it becomes a hundred dollars; later, it becomes a thousand dollars. Like that, the bickering and big fights that you have in a relationship store up and leave scars on your heart. As much as you may forgive, understand, and let go of your differences, you still have to live with the other person. As much as you love and remain attached to the other person, many scars still form in your heart. A lot of people will deny that. They say their heart is the same as when they first met their beloved. But if they look honestly, they'll probably see a lot of scars.

Only when you turn your relationship toward the Dharma and travel together on the path will Dharma give you a clear way to forgive and forget rather than remain cold, fighting, and struggling as you have, and not just with your spouse, but with everyone—family, friends, enemies—without exception. Generally, there's no other alternative for the progress you desire to make, to freshly revive your heart with everyone. Just practically speaking, consider the relationships that don't have Dharma as a base, knowing that people quarrel even once a month. Then, by the time you get to be eighty or ninety years old, you will have had countless fights, countless quarrels, countless bruises, countless scars on your heart. No one is disputing that there are good aspects to relationships. But if you weigh the good and bad, the bad is probably stronger and heavier in nearly all cases. It's only with the Dharma and bodhicitta that a relationship will not head toward a disastrous end or to one in which you feel karmically forced into staying together.

The only cure for tremendous anger and resentment is bodhicitta. In that alone, Dharma is very practical and important. In some sense, life without the Dharma can be viewed as nothing but a catastrophe. Life with the Dharma is much more peaceful and has much less suffering. Just in taking refuge we have done a great thing for ourselves in this life. But of course, a life spent truly pursuing the path of Dharma is different from someone's life who has only taken refuge. Nevertheless, it's clear that life without the Dharma contains much more suffering and very little peace—in other words, it's a catastrophe.

In that way, we could all appreciate our lives and trust in the Dharma. Really dive deeply into the meaning of the Dharma and examine it to the level of your capability. Even if the teacher is not able to present it to you perfectly well, you can do that for yourself. *The Words of My Perfect Teacher* is a great text to have sitting on one's pillow all the time. Also, teachings such as *The Bee Story* can serve as a good reminder not to take for granted the life of the Dharma and the possibilities that are available. If you read it over and over, *The Bee Story* will probably be ten times stronger than any of the teacher's suggestions or advice about what is best for you and what's not. And, since it's just a story that you're reading and reflecting on, you're not feeling influenced by somebody you might resent. Instead, whatever changes you make are of your own accord, from your own wisdom. Maybe reading this will be of much greater benefit to you than teachers making suggestions. These days, there are hardly any teachers making truly good suggestions to their students because the teachers are a little paranoid that they're going to be accused of brainwashing them, as if they're promoting some cult. Even those people who do make suggestions and speak strongly to you may be resented because you don't want to feel that anybody is taking over your life or making decisions for you about your life. You want your life to be in your own hands.

It's especially important these days to rely on the teachings if you have the interest. Of everyone who has asked to become a student of mine and receive my guidance, there are only a few with whom I can be very honest and straightforward and really tell them what I think. With others, I have to be absolutely discreet and accommodate their thinking and views. If their views go to the left, I could give them suggestions and support them to go that way. If their intentions and effort go to the right, I have to know that's also good and to give them suggestions and support for that. It's hardly possible for me just to be direct and honest. It's not that I have to lie to students. Students most likely already know this by themselves. They know quite well whether they're open toward me, how much they can hear me, and how much they can truly appreciate if I suggest another way than their preferred interest or their passing fears.

Even those people with whom I'm very close, very respectful and trusting, still—when I'm straightforward with them—I have to check with them later to see whether it really freaked them out, or whether they heard me, or if they didn't really hear me but knew that I had good intentions. It's not that I blame this on the students because I know they are trying to do their best to be good students. In my own self-reflections and confessions, I have discovered tremendous shortcomings that I'm only now realizing. So, I can naturally expect that to be the case for students also. I don't blame them, and I don't necessarily expect them to be strong, open, and receptive.

To honestly hear what your teacher has to say, you have to be extremely strong. If you're not strong enough at the time when the teacher is speaking to you, even if you go along with the teacher, you may resent any advice. Maybe you develop some sense—from different points of view or a conventional standpoint—that the teacher has dominated your life, taken over control, or has completely driven you in a way that

26

made you end up in the place that you are. There are many complications between the teacher and the students.

But with the teachings it's simple. We have a saying for the teachings: they're called "the teacher who is always patient and inscrutable." Written teachings are *always* patient; they don't become irritated with you or get upset with you, or in any way get tired of you. At the same time, the teachings are inscrutable. Whether lifetimes or centuries change, the teachings stay the same. These days, I'm really coming to understand how important it is for people to rely more on the teachings. You can resent Patrul Rinpoche's teachings, but Patrul Rinpoche is long gone, so there's no point in resenting him. People who have a connection to his teachings will totally appreciate them, and those who don't feel that connection to him probably won't be interested.

How very fortunate it is that we have met the Three Jewels. How fortunate it is that we have the Dharma in our lives because without Dharma, life is filled with confusion, pain, and catastrophe. Life with the Dharma is much different, with more peace and less pain. Those who take Dharma into their lives much more seriously and pursue the path of the Dharma honestly experience great benefit. Those who pursue the Dharma less actively will experience much less benefit. In some ways it all depends on you, but from another aspect, it doesn't depend on you personally at all. Rather, it depends on your merit and on your karma.

Dharma is two things: the scriptures and your own realization of the scriptures. As far as the scriptures are concerned, there's nothing like *The Words of My Perfect Teacher.* You can really count on that being totally sufficient to liberate you to attain enlightenment. You can rest completely in peace if you have that on your pillow. From time to time, remind yourself not to forget the Dharma and not to take this life for granted.

We also need a story that is less formal. In that way, I think *The Bee Story* has served me tremendously well, as I hope will be the case for students. Just reading it once or twice, or even ten times, you might not get much out of it without reflecting on it. But with reflection, perhaps it will become very important to your life. What Wide Wings and Sweet Voice sing—the whole effort they put into changing their fate and how it all unfolds—contains marvelous meaning. It would be great if you could learn to recite it. The purpose is not to read *The Bee Story* and forget about it. If you do that, there's not much point to it. But if you don't forget, there can be tremendous benefit.

Recently a student told me that maybe I should send my students to other teachers or to another establishment where it's not so demanding. Then they could have a more conventional life, a more regular life, as well as have various ways of practicing the Dharma. If Patrul Rinpoche's and my style of presenting the Dharma is too harsh and too difficult, maybe that student is right. I am certainly not holding anyone back if they would like to pursue another teacher or go to another establishment where they might feel more comfortable with the spiritual path. I also told him that I can't justify nor change the lineage or its teachings. Along those lines, maybe it's not right to say very much. But if it is true that people feel caught in a kind of dichotomy of having to live in certain ways that makes their spiritual path seem too far out of reach, or they are not able to practice as the teachings suggest, then it *would* be difficult to follow exactly what the lineage says and the teachings recommend. Even during practice retreats, we have a lot of difficulties in being disciplined and persistent in practicing. It's not that anyone here today is any different.

It may be helpful for people to reflect on this story from Patrul Rinpoche and to imagine themselves either as the turquoise bee, Sweet Voice, or the golden bee, Wide Wings. Then, consider all that's written here, all that they sing to each other. See how you really feel inside, how you experience it. Unless we want to live in denial, we have to face death at some point in our life. Instead of living in denial, as practitioners we have to confront our fears honestly and truthfully. From that point of view, as much as it may be painful and difficult, doing so should help practitioners see more clearly all the different ways we are attached to this world. Reflecting in this manner can liberate us and give us a sense of the pointlessness of being so attached and suffering from those very attachments.

All of the various fears we have in this life are still very small concerns, relatively speaking. The main fear that strikes everyone is their own end of life and their death. In theory, if you put yourself into the position of Wide Wings or Sweet Voice, you're not in that place yet, so you still have the time to make changes in your life and arrange to turn toward the Dharma more fearlessly. When life does come to an end, you will feel quite different from how you feel now about yourself and your practice. Your confidence in yourself and in your practice will have grown. So, it's helpful to play out this drama in your mind, with you as the actor playing Wide Wings or Sweet Voice, the golden or turquoise bee.

Also, keep in mind that truth is truth, no matter how difficult it is to face. In many of the experiences of our lives, we're not honest or truthful. If you are honest about your own weaknesses and shortcomings, you can overcome them. But if you're never truthful about them, you'll never scratch the surface to see what they truly are. Instead, you will pretend that you're the most accomplished, confident, and "together" person. In the end, be assured that other people will truly be able to see you, but you won't be able to see yourself. When that happens, ultimately, you are fooling yourself.

In this context, we're talking about one's resistance to being a Dharma practitioner and to practicing the Dharma genuinely, truthfully, and correctly. If you're truthful, even with all the different obstacles, problems, and shortcomings you have, there's nothing to feel too bad about, despite your faults, deficiencies, and difficulties. And this is true not only with us. When the buddhas and bodhisattvas of the past were in samsara, they also had to work with these same kinds of shortcomings and difficulties. So, you can confess and bring them all into the light. Once you bring them into the light and confess your faults, your weaknesses, and your failings, then there is no reason to continue feeling conflicted inside. Fear is a very natural thing for a samsaric person to feel, as well as having many faults and shortcomings. But bringing it all into the light and confessing it may be the first step toward getting rid of it.

I don't know whether anyone here today can hear this the way I mean it. When first becoming a teacher, you have all of this tradition and these goals to benefit and train others to become practitioners. Once you move in that direction and actually become a teacher with students, for a while you're confronted with people's karma and individualistic minds. At a certain point, you don't even know what to say or what not to say. Anything you may say or suggest might be completely inappropriate and unhelpful. Sometimes, it may even seem to someone like the opposite of being helpful. It's certainly not the teacher's intention to say anything that causes anyone agony, but it might actually turn out that way.

Nonetheless, the teachings are very clear. Reading this drama, you'll find everything is very clear. Many here have studied the Madhyamika teachings and understand the logic and meaning quite well. If people say they really wish to study, hear, and contemplate these teachings and take them into their hearts, this is not a very difficult thing to do. In fact, it's a piece of cake! But if people *don't* want to do that in the first place, they're probably not going to reconsider their position based on what they read here. Perhaps such people may think this view is not relevant to their life, and then just completely ignore this perspective and move on. But if you reflect deeply and repeatedly on this story, the teachings here could be helpful to you. They have been a great help to me in my personal life in making certain changes and moving in the direction that I always aim to pursue.

Part I: Text & Commentary

First, Patrul Rinpoche pays homage to Manjushri:

> Om Vajra Tiksna.
> Manjushri, Wisdom-being,
> Who plants the victory banner of the Dharma,
> Renowned for auspiciousness, virtues, and fame,
> Auspiciousness of all the auspiciousnesses, please protect me.

Here, Patrul Rinpoche is saying that the victorious Jampal Yang (Tibetan for Manjushri) provides all the auspicious circumstances in the three universes. Paying homage to Manjushri, Patrul Rinpoche expresses the aspiration that this story will be beneficial and meaningful to those who come in contact with it.

> At one time, blessed by the sole divinity, Water Lotus, touched by the feet of the Ascetic Lotus King, in the country inhabited by Tara Pemo Yogini herself, in the forest on the wide face of the mountain Lofty Lotus Peak, in the White Crystal Lotus Cave, like the rising moon, in that

place there lived a Brahman boy known as Lotus Joy who came from the Flower Garden of the Northern Plain.

He was all-knowing, wandering everywhere, living anywhere, and harmonious with everyone. He was training in the activities of the Sons of the Victors [Bodhisattvas] known as the meditation of Lotuslike Stainlessness. He was meditating on the mind of enlightenment known as Passionless Water Lotus.

This specific place, as well as the whole country of Tibet, was blessed by Avalokiteshvara. This particular location was also blessed by Tara. I believe there is a cave that has the appearance of a half-moon, and in that cave lived this Brahman boy. *Brahman* here doesn't refer to the Hindu Brahman but means "someone who abides in truth." This Brahman boy is actually a representation of Patrul Rinpoche himself, whose main practice throughout his life was the practice of bodhicitta. Bodhicitta is sometimes known as the practice of a lotus. It is "stainless" because the lotus, though it germinates in dirty water, is not stained by the mud or water. Like that, although a person who practices bodhicitta may *look* like an ordinary person, they are actually not stained by the samsaric mind or samsaric activities.

At that time, not far from that place, there was a garden called the Pleasure Garden of Lotus Heaps, a meadow flat as a mirror, surrounded by a wall of trees, a garden of blossoming lotuses, filled with tall lotuses with straight stems, blossoming lotuses with wide petals, ripe lotuses with many sweet anthers, well-arrayed lotuses with large petals, unripe lotuses with blooming sprouts, closed lotuses with folded petals, decayed lotuses with no pistils, emptied lotuses barren of pollen, worn-out lotuses with fallen petals, smiling lotuses exhibiting their pistils, hiding lotuses remaining in their coverings, and naturally ripened lotuses ready to bloom.

These lotuses represent the different people who actually surrounded the couple on whom these characters are based, or those who were part of their household.

Among them, there were three extraordinary lotuses; full, ripened, and well-arrayed. Of those three, two were fully blossomed and one was especially full and well-arrayed, but they were enjoyed by no one.

There are three lotuses that are unique. These lotuses represent those who were involved in the courtship of this couple, the main characters.

Then, in that pleasure garden, there were many swarms of honeybees zooming and playing. In particular, a tiny golden honeybee named Wide Lotus Wings and a tiny turquoise honeybee named Sweet Lotus Voice lived together as mates. The golden honeybee possessed youth, vitality, a bright intellect, and a broad mind; not anxious for new friends, he had a relaxed nature and was generous.

These are the qualities of the male bee, the golden bee. They are qualities that people respected and appreciated in the Kingdom of Derge, as well as throughout the world.

The turquoise bee was also greatly able to give, with a beneficial mind and a tender nature; devoted to Dharma, she had little deceit, envy, or jealousy. These two, with affection for each other, lived together with smiling faces, loving words, and a harmonious way of life. In confidence they shared their minds' wishes with each other.

These are the two bees who confidently made this aspiration together, begun by Wide Wings, the golden bee, and continuing in the song that he sings to his mate, the turquoise bee.

Wide Wings said:

Oh, how delightful is the flower of youth.
It is not painted by the brush strokes of the Creator of
Prosperity [God],
But produced by the illusory display of virtuous deeds.
Is it not even able to compete with the gods within the
gods' realms?

The glory of enjoyments is not accumulated by ourselves,
But it appears because of the power of former deeds.
The tender seats of flowers are not woven.
The tender touch is their own property from the beginning.
The sweetness of the pistil is not prepared.
This drink of one hundred tastes is an immortal nectar.

Here he is saying that a flower still in its youth is bright and vivid, and even more incredibly, that it is not a painting created by some supernatural painter, but is actually real. It is not produced by the God who is thought to be the creator of all the world—a theistic world—but is created through virtuous deeds. He is referring to the beauty of the kingdom, as well as the wealth and prosperity they possess.

> The glory of happiness and joy does not arrive because of exertions.
> It is accomplished naturally because of former accumulated merit.
> If you can apply the mind's intention to the Dharma,
> Then your own body is worthy to be called the body of freedom and endowments.
> However, toward the state of those human beings accomplishing evil deeds,
> Although they can speak and understand, it is not worthy to make aspirations.

They realize all that they possess in their domain is due to their good karma from the past. It is not that they have striven so hard in this life. For example, being born in a noble family is not something that you strive for on your own. It has to come from your karma. Then he says that in this beautiful life they share, if they would just put their mind toward the Dharma and embrace it, they could wholly proclaim that they have a precious human birth. He also states that he doesn't have much of an aspiration to follow others who may seem to be very powerful and influential but who strive to achieve their aims through negative deeds.

> O, listen, my delightful sweetheart.
> Here, the flower garden is splendid,
> The taste and nutriment of the sweet nectar is rich,
> The swarms of harmonious-voiced bees are numerous.
> But the glory of the summer months is momentary,
> The numerous causes of death are sudden,

The changes of happiness and suffering are instantaneous,
The escort of the Lord of Death comes closer and closer.

This is self-explanatory; he speaks his mind regarding the
impermanence of all things. Also, he has the aspiration
to practice the Dharma, and because of his awareness of
impermanence, he genuinely wants his mate to hear and
practice Dharma as well.

If we waste our lives in the desire for happiness,
Then the happiness of this life will have no essence.
Concerning the distractions of the so-called engagement in
samsaric activities,
There is no end, now and in the future.
Even if efforts are made for this life's living arrangements
for a long time,
There is no essence if the life span becomes exhausted.
Even though the appearance of this flower garden is comfortable,
If we must separate, then there is no benefit.
Reflect on this meaning and resolve your mind.
My loving companion, let us follow the Dharma path.
My fortunate friend, I aspire to the holy Dharma.
My heart-friend, do you feel the same?

He gets agreement from his sweetheart, and she responds.

At this, Sweet Voice said:

Excellent, excellent; sweetheart, you are right!
Your heart-words, the support of my mind, are right,
The words of your heart poured as the essence of my heart
Are my heart's nectar of immortality.

His mind and her mind are totally linked and become one at
this point.

It is not invited here from the land of the Gods.
The delightful flower garden of the land of men,
The wealth of the fortunate and harmonious bees,
Provides great joy because of previous deeds.

She states how beautiful the land is and that everything they have is comparable to the wealth and the beauty of the god realm. It almost seems as though this god realm has descended to the earth.

Although beautiful, it is impermanent, the character of samsara.
Although prosperous, it is impermanent, the wealth of illusion.
Although enjoyed, it is dissatisfying, the deception of wealth.
Essenceless is the realm of samsara.

As for you, put armor on your mind.
I also will draw the same picture in my heart.
How can we change our firm decision?
We, fortunate friends, will follow the path of Dharma.

She means that if they can firmly hold this conviction, then Wide Wings can prepare his mind to picture it and also move in that direction. If they both make that decision, without wavering, then they are sure to achieve the accomplishment.

Hoarded wealth has no essence.
Even though seeking it through efforts,
Wealth will be enjoyed by others.
Cherished retinues have no essence.
Although they are cared for with kindness, it becomes an invitation to animosity.
Constructed castles have no essence.
Although intended to be beneficial, they become the rolling stone that cuts off life.
Cultivated fields have no essence.

Although counted as excellent, they become the
slaughterhouses of insects.

Yet we should proceed slowly.
Hurried activities will not reach their end.
Let us write these heart-promises in our hearts.
No one but ourselves has greater control over our own minds.

So, she responds quite positively, without being distracted.

Next is a representation of the sage Lama Akar, whom they go
to see, and whose instructions follow here.

At that time there was a sage known as the All-
Accomplished One [Don-Kun Grub-Pa] who had a
peaceful bearing, a loving heart, and especially delighted
in serving beings. And he came to that land. The two bees
arrived near him and bowed with respect. They offered the
sweet-tasting honey. Commencing with polite speech they
prayed to him:

O great holy sage! You are the regent of the Teacher
[Buddha]. Therefore, please give a teaching in accordance
with the precepts of the Buddha. You are the torch of
the doctrine, therefore please give an essential teaching
on practice. You are a member of the noble community
[Sangha], therefore please explain the way of life of the
Buddha's sons. We also will follow after you, Holy One.

Having heard their prayer thus, the countenance of that
great Sage glowed with the effulgence of his mind. He
displayed the splendor of his body. He expressed the
resonance of his speech, speaking the Dharma thus:

Homage to the Noble Holy One!
To the Protector, the God of the Gods,

The Excellent One among human beings,
the Peerless Guide who leads living beings,
The Excellent being born in the Sakyan race, I bow down.
Please turn the minds of the beings of the six realms to
the Dharma.

O two bees, you who are related to me by previous karma[1],
If you seek the Dharma path from the heart,
then reflect on this meaning.
These are the precepts of the Buddha, so think about
their purpose.
This is the very essence of the Dharma, so keep it in your minds.
Ema![2] Living beings of the six classes
From past times have wandered long in the realm of samsara.
In the future there will be no exhaustion of the illusory
appearances of karma and defilements.
For tens of millions of eons, beyond calculation,
It is difficult even to hear the names of the Three Jewels.
Therefore, to meet the Buddha's teachings is like seeing a
star in daytime.

In this age, the Fourth Leader [Buddha], the son of Suddhodhana,
The Excellent Leader, the Lord of Sages, came to this world.
He turned the three successive wheels of the Dharma.
The duration of the doctrine, the tenfold five-hundred-year period,
has not yet become exhausted.
At this time, when one has the desire for seeking the
Dharma path and
Possesses the favorable circumstances of being accepted
by a virtuous friend [teacher],
If you do not seek the Dharma path from the heart,
In the future you will not take rebirth in this kind of land.
Even hearing the name of the Three Jewels will be difficult.

Ema, worldly beings who wander within illusory appearances
Apprehend the essenceless composite phenomena as eternal.

However, the realm of the elements of the outer world is impermanent.
The lives of the living beings, the contained, are impermanent.
In between, the glory of the seasons and months is impermanent.
Even those holy beings, the Buddha and his sons, are impermanent.
Look at their demonstration of the way of entering
cessation [nirvana].
For the Master of Beings, the Lord of Brahmas, the
greatest within existence [samsara],
There is no need to say that they will be lassoed by the
noose of the Lord of Death.
No one has certainty of when and where one will die.
There are many causes of death and very few causes of life.
Therefore, you should seek the Dharma path quickly,
Otherwise, it is uncertain when the Lord of Death will arrive, and
All beings are certain to die like animals in a slaughterhouse.

Ema, after death one will not disappear,
But one will transmigrate and take birth in this realm of samsara.
Wherever one is born there is no opportunity for happiness.
In the eighteen hell realms beings are tormented by the
suffering of burning and freezing,
In the hungry-ghost realm by hunger and thirst, and in
the animal realm by eating each other.
Human beings are tormented by short lives and
demigods by fighting and struggling,
Gods by careless distraction, dying, and falling.
There is no happiness anywhere, but a pit of fire everywhere.
In birth and the succession of lives, beings wander,
suffering continuously.
You must develop revulsion for the phenomena of
cyclical existence.

Ema, happiness and suffering are created by karma.
Karma is the creator of all things, like a painter.
Karma ripens without being exhausted even after one
hundred eons.

Karma produced by oneself will not change and
will not be experienced by another.
Virtuous karma produces happiness and birth in high
realms and liberation.
Unvirtuous karma produces suffering and rebirth in inferior
realms and samsara.
Even if the cause is small, it produces a great result.
The glory, prosperity, joy, and happiness of the gods, the
high realms, and
The unbearable sufferings of hell, the inferior realms,
Are created by nothing else but one's own karma.
Therefore at all times and in all circumstances,
Establish recollection, mindfulness, and alertness as the basis.
Exert yourselves earnestly in the right way of accepting
and rejecting causes and effects.

Ema, the excellent torch that guides one on the path of liberation,
The source of all the qualities, the virtuous friend [teacher],
Performs the actions of the actual Buddha in this dark age.
His compassion and graciousness are immeasurable,
greater than that of the Buddhas.
If you do not have a perfect, virtuous friend,
Then you are like a blind man entering a path without a support.
Therefore, this wish-fulfilling gem, this wish-granting tree,
The holy master—first examine him and then take him as
a teacher.
Finally learn his activities and thoughts, and unify your
mind with his.

This kind of fortunate disciple will not fall under the
control of the devil, and
He will obtain the excellent path pleasing to the Buddhas.

Ema, the abode of nirvana, peace and bliss,
Is the Dharma, free from all the diseases of samsara,

The total perfection of the exhaustion of suffering together
with its causes,
The holy city, liberated together with its uncontaminated paths,
Fully filled with the riches of the Victors and the Sons of
the Victors, and
The place of delight for the Noble Ones, the Hearers, and
Self-enlightened Ones.
It is proper to seek this path of liberation.

Ema, the perpetual, infallible, holy protectors,
The peerless Precious Jewels possessing graciousness—
I am satisfied by seeking refuge in them.
It is proper for you also to seek refuge in them.
If you take refuge with belief and respect from the heart,
There is no equal to the Three Jewels, infallible
throughout all time.
The Three Jewels are capable of protecting from the
sufferings of samsara.
The merits of taking refuge are equal to the limits of space.
In this life, the eight and sixteen fears, and so forth—
The complete mass of unfavorable evil—will be removed.
In the next life, it is certain that you will be liberated from
All the suffering of an inferior being revolving in the inferior realms.
Therefore, always remember the Triple Gem,
Go for refuge again and again, and recite prayers.

Ema, the trial of progress of the numerous Buddhas,
The sole path of progress of the Buddha's sons,
The peerless jewel, the excellent Mind of Enlightenment,
With its aspects of aspiration and entering, please develop.
From this you will obtain the name of the Son of the Victors.
You will proceed from the path of bliss to the field of bliss.
Attainment of perfect, full Buddhahood is not far away.
The beings of the three worlds are your kind parents.
They are like a protectorless and friendless blind man
wandering in a field.

Although desiring happiness they indulge in the causes of suffering.
By composing the mind in love and compassion for them,
Thinking to dispel the suffering of all beings by yourself,
Attire yourself in the armor of this great, inconceivable mind.
Meditate on the equality of self and others,
the exchange of self with others, and
the view that others are more dear than yourself.
Practice with exertion from the heart
the four boundless states of mind, the six perfections,
and the four means of attraction of disciples.
It is said that the complete activities of the Sons of the Victors
Are completed in the excellent path of the six perfections.
This perfect, excellent path, pleasing to the Buddhas,
Is the essence of the heart, so keep it in the center of your heart.

Ema, the duration of living in the dwelling of samsara is long.
From beginningless time we have gravely accumulated evil deeds.
Therefore, by the application of the complete four
powers [*s Tobs-bZhi*],
If one does not cultivate this skillful means
of confession of evil deeds and falls from the precepts,
It will be difficult to be liberated from the inferior realms
of samsara.
The sole body of all the Bliss-gone Buddhas,
According to the jewel method [tradition] condensing
all the root and lineage Lamas;
Vajrasattva, white like the color of the conch shell and moon,
Seated upon a white lotus and moon with a smiling face:
If you visualize him and recite the hundred syllables
according to the liturgy,
Then you will destroy all effects of evil deeds and falls from
the precepts, and
Stir [empty] the depths of all the realms of hell.

Ema, Buddhahood is for those who have completed
the accumulations of merit and wisdom.

45

There is no chance of accomplishment for those who have not completed the accumulations.
Therefore, as a skillful means, offer the collected assemblage of wealth and
The Buddha Lands manifested by mind.
Visualizing the triple thousand Nirmanakaya pure lands, the unexcelled Sambhogakaya pure lands, and
The ultimate nature Dharmakaya pure land;
With your body, wealth, and virtues of the three times,
Offer these to the divine Lama, to the Three Jewels, and to the three Bodies.
From this, merit will be completed and one's perceptions of Buddha fields will be perfected.
The minds of beings will be ripened and the merit will be infinite.
Therefore, I accept the accumulations as the heart of the instructions.

Ema, from beginningless time, due to ignorance,
Beings wander in samsara by apprehending that which is selfless to be the self.
Desire and hatred arise through clinging
to the nonexistent body, assuming it to be the body.
Therefore, this cherished illusory body,
Dedicate as the substance of offering and giving without attachment.
In the form of nectar offer upward to the Three Jewels, and
Give downward to the beings of the six realms.
They will be satisfied and your dual accumulations will be perfected.
All your karmic debts will be paid, obstructing and harmful spirits will be satisfied, and obstructions will be pacified.
All substances of offerings manifested by mind and all necessary wealth,
Offer upward and give downward and dedicate the merit for the sake of all beings.
All phenomena are merely different varieties of thought.
So this merit is equal to giving your own body directly.
It establishes the habit of great generosity.
It completes the merit, purifies obscurations, and causes the

realization of the clarity of the intermediate state.
It ransoms death and reverses sickness, obstructions, and
harmful forces.
Therefore this is a skillful means for the accumulation of merit.

Ema, the embodiment of the Three Jewels possessing kindness,
The essence of all the Buddhas, the precious one,
The holder of the treasure of teachings of the three
transmissions, the blessed one:
The supreme guide, the root Lama—pray to him or her.
If you visualize the Lama on the crown of your head or in
the center of your heart,
The merit is equal to visualizing all the Bliss-gone Buddhas.
The blessings of the Lamas of the three transmissions will
enter into your own mind.
The Lama's mind and your mind will mix inseparably and
realization will arise.
Therefore, for the most excellent method of progress
in realization of the ultimate nature,
Guru Yoga is the profound essence.
Receive the four initiations from the lights of the letters in
the three places.
Establish the capacity for purifying the four obscurations,
Attaining the levels of four bodies and the level of
Knowledge-holder of the four classes.
You will then attain the potential to practice
the four paths and will restore the decay of the sacred vows.
All the phenomena of samsara and nirvana will arise as the
play of the Lama.
For the time being unfavorable circumstances will be
pacified and wishes fulfilled.
Ultimately in this life you will secure the reign of Dharmakaya.
Even if not, in the next life you will be reborn in the land of
Lotus Light.
In that land, from progressing through the path of the four
Knowledge-holders,

You will enter into the primordial sphere like an illusion.
You will serve the purposes of beings equal to the limits of space.
The appearances of bodies and wisdom will fill
phenomenal existence.

Ema, these are the sole paths of progress of all the Buddhas,
The oral precepts of the lineage of the Knowledge-holders
of the three transmissions,
The condensation of the sutras of the eighty-four thousand
sacred Dharmas are
The crucial essence of the instructions!
Even if one hundred learned ones and one thousand saints
should arrive,
There will be no one who teaches a more profound Dharma
than this.
This is the inner essence of the sacred Dharma nectar.
This is the main practice of the thousands of the Sangha,
the holy assemblage.
By whatever merits are obtained through preaching and
listening to this path,
May all the endless living beings,
Relying on this excellent path, in a single lifetime
Achieve fully perfected enlightenment.

This is the teaching on the ngöndro practice—the outer
preliminary practice and the inner preliminary practice—
condensed here in phrases, with its essence laid out. Most
people in Tibet and those here have studied the ngöndro, so if
you look at it carefully, you will understand. We won't go into
the details of the explanation of ngöndro now. Besides, no one
can explain it any better than *The Words of My Perfect Teacher*.

After speaking thus, he gave blessings and said aspirations
for the two bees. By wandering, he fulfilled the needs
of living beings, of whoever saw, heard, remembered, or
touched him. Then in the hermitage known as Medicinal

48

Eye Drops he attained complete nirvana in the state of no residue of body, like the exhaustion of the fuel of a fire.

Then, for a long time, the two bees followed their daily lives mostly in accordance with the teachings of the sage, but sometimes they played carelessly with attachment to the objects of desire. Once, while Sweet Voice was drinking the sweet essence of the flowers and Wide Wings was flying around in the sky, the light color of the sun suddenly faded. The shadow of the dark clouds fell on the ground. The flowers simultaneously closed their mouths. Sweet Voice was enclosed within the flower. Suffocating, filled with fear and unable to speak, she remained trapped within, uttering "Bub Bub Bub Bub." Wide Wings, also filled with fear and helplessness, landed at the foot of the flower.

What actually happened to the real couple in Tibet is that the woman got smallpox and had to be quarantined. Because smallpox was so contagious and dangerous, she couldn't be in contact with anyone since there was no immunization or cure available at the time.

His heart suppressed by torments of suffering, he rolled on the ground and said:

Alas, alas, how fearful and scary!
Oh, Oh, what a sudden misfortune!
What to do, what to do with this cruel violence?
Which devil has arrived here so suddenly?
The enchanting disk of the sun in the sky,
who is the ferocious one who has covered it so suddenly?
The one-hundred-petaled flowers arrayed on the ground,
What bad circumstances have terminated their lives so suddenly?
My charming, sweetheart companion, where have you gone?
My tender, wide-winged, moving one, where have you gone?
My emitter of sweet songs, where have you gone?

My confidante of love, where have you gone?
My beautiful, smiling one, where have you gone?
My delightful, buzzing one, where have you gone?
My turquoise, fuzzed one with slanting glances, where
have you gone?

The phrase "slanting glances" might not sound as beautiful
in English, but at that time it was a very poetic way to
describe women in India or Tibet because generally they were
considered to possess the ornaments of humility and shyness.
Such women would never look directly into a man's face or
eyes; they looked at them sideways, which was said to be very
penetrating to a lover, so that's why it's described this way here.

My beautiful six-legged one, where have you gone?
My shining, spotted one, where have you gone?
My black, rich hair-knotted one, where have you gone?
Piece of my own heart, where have you gone?
Wide Wing's inside is empty; what to do?
Get up, get up! Can you hear, beloved Sweet Voice?
If there is no answer to Wide Wing's plea,
Then my heart will be near to splitting in pieces.

O sudden dark cloud without pity, what is this catastrophe
for the innocent bees?
O gracious, wide, one-hundred-petaled flower, don't you
have any independence?

All-beneficial sun, master of compassion,
please don't remain behind the furious dark cloud.
Please send forth your light rays and heat of compassion.
If I were Vayabe [the wind] I would be joyous
that the storm was dispersing the furious black cloud.
If I were a two-legged human I would be happy
with the power to open one hundred wide flowers.
Alas, high sky, do you pay attention to this kind of fate of

the humble bee?
Please issue a command to the furious dark clouds.

Sweet Voice, Sweet Voice, essence of my heart,
Sweet Voice, Sweet Voice, vine of my heart,
Sweet Voice, Sweet Voice, loving companion,
Sweet Voice, Sweet Voice, my beloved goddess, alas, alas!

Wide Wings is in a very depressed state when Sweet Voice
becomes trapped. Similarly, the man whose lover was
quarantined with small pox could only communicate with her
from outside a closed door and at some distance. She was not
able to come out, nor could he go in. He desperately wanted to,
but everyone stopped him. This is a crucial part of the story.

Sad Wide Wings said this, rolling on the ground in total
exhaustion. In that place, when she caught her breath a
little bit, Sweet Voice was able slowly to utter a cry. From

the middle of the flower she called out: "Wide Wings, Wide Wings." Then, Wide Wings became very happy, thinking that Sweet Voice had revived. He stood up quickly and, facing the flower closely, cried out, "Sweet Voice."

This is the essence of the story for us to reflect on.

At that time, Sweet Voice heard the crying voice of Wide Wings. She realized that she was trapped within the middle of the flower and considered the situation precisely. She thought:

"Oh no, although we two have formerly heard all the profound teachings from the Great Sage known as Accomplishing the Welfare of All, we have not practiced even a little. Although we made the promise and had the determination to practice the pure, holy Dharma, my life has become exhausted in the state of merely wishing to practice Dharma. Now I must die enclosed within the middle of this flower after having experienced for a long time suffering like the decline and fall of the gods. Or will it be possible that, being touched by the rays of the sun, the one-hundred-petaled flower will open and I will be delivered before death arrives? Either way, Wide Wings is depressed by sorrow and if I give an answer he might hear."

At this point, Wide Wings realizes that Sweet Voice is trapped inside the flower. Wide Wings feels frightened because he recognizes that Sweet Voice might die within the flower, leaving him behind. Sweet Voice also realizes that although she had received many teachings, she had not put them into practice enough to develop the confidence in herself to pursue the path further.

This is a situation we will all face. Just as it happens to Sweet Voice in this story, it will happen to all of us. When we fall upon our deathbed, this is exactly the situation we will go through. Since it's a situation that will occur in our own life, similarly, we need to reflect.

She said:

O, O, Wide Wings, O, O, Wide Wings,
Excellent Wide Wings, divine prince,
After hearing your charming sweet voice, nectar of the ears,
I have joy in my heart; but this youthful, handsome face,
The nectar of the eyes, what a misfortune that I cannot see it.

The sudden dark messenger of the Lord of Death,
I do not know when he will arrive.
Beneficial to all, the creator of the day, the orb of light,
Without remaining in the sky, where did it go?

The decorative bedding of petals, soft to the touch,
The dripping essence of nectar, sweet to the taste,
The ambrosia of the nose, sweetly fragrant to the smell,
The youthfulness of white and red flowers, the joyful
celebration for the eyes,
The assembly of flowers, the enjoyment of all wishes,
How did it become a murdering executioner?
The hundreds of thin, soft petals becoming a vicious prison, and
The sweet wealth becoming binding chains
Is the character of the suffering of change.

Here, she is talking about how the flowers she used to enjoy through each one of her senses have completely changed now that she sees them as the very cause of her death.

O! When the great, kind sage
Gave the nectar-like instructions,
He said that impermanence was the characteristic of samsara.
Today it is apparent to us.
Although my enjoyments competed with the prosperity of the gods,

53

To arrive exhausted at the gates of the Lord of Death
Did not take more than a blink of my eyes.
Alas, the suffering of death is like this.

Although I had in mind the desire to practice the
divine Dharma,
I was unable to immediately endeavor in practice.
If I must proceed on the long, narrow path of the
intermediate state,
I will not have any sacred Dharma attainment on which to rely.

Although the thought of death's coming was in my mind,
While being careless, indifferent, and lazy,
The demon Lord of Death has suddenly arrived.

Although I had in my mind the suffering of samsara,
I could not cut off the attachment to the joys of
adventitious appearances.
Through the five faculties being deceived by the five devils
of the objects,
The basis of the suffering of samsara has been established.
Although the belief in the infallibility of cause and effect
was in my mind,
I could not practice their profound acceptance and rejection.
Having exhausted life in the state of distraction,
I have no reliance on the practice of virtue.

O my youthful sweetheart bee,
There is a fearful enemy, the Demon Lord of Death,
Of whom I have formerly heard.
Now he has arrived in person.

Regarding a dwelling place,
I don't have in my heart the desire to leave the flower garden,
But now suddenly by the Lordly King of Death
I am being led to the city gates of the Lord of Death.

Regarding food to eat,
Although in my mind I don't have the desire to abandon
the sweet honey,
By the law of the powerful one, powerless, I must eat the
burnt smell as food.

Regarding the path of travel,
Except for the wide sky I don't have the desire to land
anywhere else,
But now taken by the Lord of Death, powerless,
It seems necessary to wander on the narrow path of the
intermediate state.

Regarding loving relations,
Although I don't want to separate from my gracious
mother and father,
Now in the court of the King of the Law,
Relationless and friendless, it seems I must wander.

Regarding my cherished retinue, my friends the honeybees,
Although I don't wish to be separated from them,
Now from taking the great road of the next life,
Friendless and alone, it seems I must wander.

Regarding clothing to wear,
Although in my mind I don't wish to abandon the soft and
tender cotton,
Now bound by the noose of the Lord of Death,
Naked without clothing it seems I am led.

Regarding my companion and friend, the golden bee Wide Wings,
Although in my mind I don't wish to separate from him,
Now due to the faults of compound phenomena being
demonstrated,
It seems he will disappear from my sight and hearing.

O my handsome and youthful sweetheart,
From our first companionship to now,
Your beautiful face has been adorned with loving smiles.
I don't remember angry frowns.

Sweet Voice, cared for with words of love,
does not remember your giving wrathful scoldings.
Excellent nature of companionship with a loving heart,
I don't remember any shameless fickleness in you.

Regarding immediate wealth, necessities,
I don't remember your making distinctions between me and yourself.
For the long duration of our lives together I don't recall any
unpleasant behavior.

The kindness of your caring for me
With a heart of excellent nature and loyalty is in my mind.
The affection of your companionship
Of uninterrupted love for me is in my mind.
The words of love of your enchanting and
Harmonious speech is in my mind.
The affectionate devotion of your
Ceaseless intimate heart is in my mind.

Although it seems I shall now be leaving my dwelling place,
I do not grieve from thinking about my land or my place.
Although it seems I shall now be separated from my
amassed wealth,
I do not grieve from thinking about my abundance and wealth.
Although it seems that I shall now be separated from my
cherished servants,
I do not grieve from thinking about my attending servants
and deputies.
Although it seems I shall now be separated from my cherished body,
I do not grieve from thinking about my youthful age.
Although it seems that I shall be separated from my dear life,

I do not grieve from remembering the joy of this life.

But the suffering of inevitable separation
From you, my sweetheart cared for with love, pierces the heart.
There is no means to console my grief.
From remembering the beauty of your lovely face,
An incessant rain of tears falls from my eyes.
From remembering the attention of your loving heart,
The darkness of sorrow covers my mind.
From remembering the inspiration of your loving words,
The flame of sadness burns in my mind.

But what can I do? The forces of karma have arrived.
Who can repulse the forces of the Lord of Death?
Who can prevent the appearances of suffering samsara?
You also, from thinking about this nature,
I beg you not to grieve.

Still, if the light rays of the sun arise,
There is the possibility of my being freed.
Please relax and remain optimistic.

Even if I cannot escape, and I die here,
There is nothing more you could have done in the past
Regarding loving care and affection, you, my heart-friend,
Who accompanied me with love. So the wishes of my life's
end are fulfilled.

In the past when we were happy,
The promises of our wishes were written in our hearts.
Now do you remember in your heart, excellent one?
In the future even if the time of our separation arrives,
Please do not abandon your heart-vow.
If you could concentrate your mind and fulfill the training
in holy Dharma,
There is nothing else to request from you than this.

Then Wide Wings said:

O Sweet Voice, O Sweet Voice,
Sweet Voice, my little singing turquoise bee,
Do not be afraid or fear but relax.
Do not be frightened or terrified but be courageous of mind.
Temporary situations do not last for a long time.
The dark clouds in the sky do not remain in one place.
It is impossible for the sun's light to fade.
The sudden dark clouds, this sudden unfortunate obstacle,
There may be a way to dispel it.

Our large circle of cherished insects, bees, and worms,
If we send them as messengers in all directions,
We will be able to accomplish the wishes sought by our hearts.
The treasure of honey, our accumulated wealth,
If we were able to give it as charity, would dispel our
sudden disaster.
If we inquire from the wise and learned ones of the world,
We would know the means to avert the cause and
conditions of our sudden disaster.
If we rely on others endowed with power and strength,
It would avert the face of the sudden dark cloud.

This exactly parallels what happened when the lady was ill with
smallpox and placed in quarantine. The minister sent all his
attendants and servants throughout the Kingdom of Derge to
consult with different lamas, hermits, and powerful magicians,
seeking predictions and rituals that might help. Each animal
represents a specific lama or another actual person.

In unfixed nests in hamlets and rock mountains,
The small, black raven caws
And, it is said, gives predictions to the entire world.
If we ask him, he will give prophecies.

On the roofs of the lofty fortresses,
There is assembled a great flock of sparrows.
It is said that they recite the dharani of Vajra Vidarana.
If we invite this flock they may perform propitiations.

In the midst of the wetness of ponds and springs,
There are frogs ugly in appearance.
It is said that they are messengers of black Mara Naga.
If we ask them, they may have a way.

In the midst of leaves at the foot of trees and in holes,
There are black, venomous snakes revealing dreaded forms.
It is said that they possess the very form of the poisonous
Lord of Water.
If we take refuge in them, the dark clouds will be averted.

In the abode of the mountaintop earthen burrows,
There are great, marmot meditators, meditating for a long time.

This must be me! [Rinpoche chuckles.]

It is said that they possess the concentration to accomplish
the absorptions.
If we ask them, they will grant heart blessings.

On the top of the branches of enchanting trees,
There are turquoise cuckoos emitting sweet songs.
It is said that they are the emissarial voices inviting the
rain clouds.
If we serve them they will silence their voices.

In the enchanting meadows of the northern plains,
Are the divine messengers, the small, wild, white-muzzled horses.
It is said that they possess a jewel invoking the sun's rays.
If we ask them, they will raise their muzzles.

In its own hole and in other uncertain places,
Is a nine-legged black spider, the killer of all.
It is said that he is the manifestation of a black Dolpa.
If we approach him, he will make arrangements.

From the sky, on the bare-rocked mountain tops,
Are brownish kites emitting screeches.
It is said that they are messengers of the King of Eagles.
If we rely on them, they will show their wrathful actions.

It is impossible to have a disaster that cannot be overcome
by some means.
It is impossible to have an evil deed that cannot be cleansed
by confession.
It is impossible to have an obstruction that cannot be
subdued by antidotes.
It is impossible to have a demonic obstruction without a
means of reversal.
The golden bee Wide Wings has ideas and methods.
In this spacious place I have complete independence.
I must try whichever of the hundred methods is better and effective.

So now Wide Wings approaches the raven, who is thought to
have clairvoyance, allowing him to predict things.

Having said this, Wide Wings approached the raven who said:

The source is the Naga, the remedy is the Garuda.
The antidote is the wind; there are many methods of reversal.
Although it is stormy now, there will be no ill effects in the end.

Likewise Wide Wings visited all the others. The chief of
the flock of sparrows said:

This would actually be the head of the monastery, a monk who
is in charge of the assembly.

The blessings of this assemblage are like a force of flames.
Since it is able to burn the forest of former evil deeds,
What need is there to mention a clump of adventitious circumstances?
But careful offerings and services are necessary.

Having said this, the sparrow came and performed propitiations.
The frog said:

I, the frog, exhibiting ugliness,
Am the messenger of the Black Demon Naga.
The barbarous Naga is the source of the black cloud.
If I ask him, he will certainly be able to disperse it.

Having said this, the frog positioned himself, staring at the sky.
The serpent said:

From the fangs of the wrathful Lord of the Water
Arise steam, clouds, and hail.
Just as the snake possesses vicious fangs,
so I have the means to clear away the black cloud.

Having said this, the serpent slithered around.
The marmot said:

I contemplate on the absorptions without distraction.
But because the golden bee's presence is so compelling,
I will surely perform long-life prayers from my meditation burrow.
It is certain that in the end there will be no harm.

Having said this, the marmot sat with half-closed eyes.
The cuckoo said:

The rainclouds are the emissaries of the gods.
Their messenger is the blue cuckoo.
I have a little power over their movements.
Of course I will do my best.

Having said this, the cuckoo sat flexing his body.
The wild horse said:

I am the small, wild, grey stallion.
My upper muzzle is the wish-fulfilling jewel.
It is the broom clearing the covering of the sky.
You did not make a mistake in coming to me.

Having said this, the wild horse raised his upper muzzle
to the sky.
The black spider said:

The breath of the vicious, barbarous Naga
Is not able to be cleared by other means.
If the flesh of insects and flies is gathered,
I will perform the offering liberating the harmful spirits.

Having said this, he weaved many threaded masts.
The kite said:

I myself am the great Garuda, who subdues the Nagas.
I eat snakes, gobble up frogs, and destroy the wealth
of the Nagas.
The power of my talons is like thunder.
I will destroy the Nagas into atoms by means of my
wrathful actions.

Having spoken these words, the kite soared in the sky
and screeched.

Now, here is what happens. When one's time comes, one has to
go. As Guru Rinpoche said, even if it is the Medicine Buddha
himself, nothing can be done. We will still have all these
hopeful thoughts and try to convince ourselves, but then it all
fails.

Then Wide Wings thought: "Judging from the explanations given by the great beings known to all, in the end the dark clouds will disappear and Sweet Voice will be liberated," and so he remained relaxed for a while. Then at that moment, the dark clouds started boiling and grimly churned in all directions. From the southern direction, the sound of thunder rumbled and the violent storm raged and howled. Simultaneously, the flower petals closed even more tightly. Enclosed within the flower, not only was Sweet Voice unable to move her arms and legs but she was suffocated and could hardly utter a sound. She said with a faint voice:

Kyema! Wide Wings, Divine Prince,
The hundred petals of the flower are tightening.
The roughness of the pistils is harsh like thorns.
The many furrows of the petals are as hard as a rock.

Enclosed, it is difficult to move my arms and legs.
Suffocating, it is difficult to inhale and exhale.
Choked up, it is difficult to speak.
Now it is certain that I shall not be freed.

From all sides the sound of thunder is rumbling.
The sudden storm is howling.
Since the flower is floating and bobbing,
The pond must be agitated and shaking.
It is certain that hail from the dark cloud will come.

When the violent hail arrives,
The growing green grass will be flattened,
The stems standing upright will break down,
The array of branches will be chopped off,
The ripened fruits will be scattered,
The blossoming flowers will be destroyed.

It will be almost as if the sky and earth are turned
upside down.
It will be almost as if the hard rock is dismantled.
It will be almost as if the tall trees are destroyed.

Fierce lightning will come.
Now it is time even for you to run away.
Sweet Voice will not be freed, it is certain.
These are the last words of separation between the living
and dying.
It is not proper to say much, but in brief:

Now she speaks from her heart of her truest desire and what's
in her mind.

The past words of the great sage,
They are sticking in my mind even more.

By this, she refers to the teachings that Lama Akar gave to them.

The words about the suffering of cyclical existence,
Now I recognize them even more.
The teaching about the impermanence of everything,
Now even more it has become manifest.
All that is gathered will certainly separate.
Do not allow your mind to be depressed,
I also will not grieve but will persevere.
Our past words, a silken knot,
Are they still tied without loosening?

This means they made a promise to do Dharma practice but
were not able to keep that commitment because they became
distracted. So, she's asking whether his mind is clear about that.

Our wishes, pictures of stone,
Are they still vivid without fading?

Our promises, the stakes of the heart,
Are they still planted without being pulled out?

In the appearances of suffering cyclical existence,
Have you developed remorse from the depth of your heart?
In the uncertainty of the time of arrival of the Lord of Death,
Do you now have definite surety in your mind?
Toward the deception of the five sense objects,
Have you reversed attachment from the depth of your heart?
In the certainty of separation of all that is composite,
Have you attained firm confidence?

Though I met the holy lord [teacher],
I regret not having cleared away my doubts.
Though I heard the excellent teachings of the holy Dharma,
I regret not having gained experience in practice.
Though I obtained a birth having freedom and endowments,
I regret not having achieved the essence.

Though I understood impermanence and death,
I regret not having accomplished the Dharma for death.
Though I heard various aspects of causes and effects,
I regret not having been able to accept and reject them appropriately.
Though the suffering of samsara was discoursed upon,
I regret not having given birth to remorse toward it.
Now death has suddenly arrived.

The frown of the Lord of Death is as black as darkness.
When his raging eyes dart about, I will be terrified.
When escorted in front by the fearful darkness,
Not finding my own way, I will be terrified.
When pursued from behind by the storm of karma,
Not obtaining freedom, I will be terrified.
When roaring like thunder, "Kill, Kill, Hit, Hit!"
Such delusory appearances arise, I will be terrified.

When the grimacing executioners of the Lord of Death
Perform their ferocious deeds, I will be terrified.
When my neck is caught by the lasso of the Lord of Death,
Powerlessly being dragged along, I will be terrified.
When transferring to the next life,
Friendless and alone, I will be terrified.

When I wander in a strange land without coming back,
Not knowing where to go, I will be terrified.
When the illusory appearances of the six realms are as
clear as stars,
Without protection and refuge, I will be terrified.

I am an example of a person who intended to practice the Dharma
But was unable to accomplish it immediately.
You, my little sweetheart bee,
Contemplate on this situation and make efforts in the
practice of the holy Dharma.

Without delaying, go to the holy Dharma.
Without wavering, commit your mind to practice.
Without deferring, bear courage in mind.
Without postponing, develop perseverance immediately.

Even facing significant difficulties, do not reject the Dharma.
Even at the cost of your life, keep your promise.
The counsels of this world are the words of demons.
Do not keep them in your mind but disregard them.
Distractions and laziness are the causes of deceiving.
Reject them as poison.

A life filled from beginning to end with Dharma,
A life connected to Dharma,
The practice of holy Dharma perfected to the end,
Maintaining security for yourself,
Achievement of the path of liberation for myself, and

Finally in the pure land of great bliss,
The direct meeting between living you and dead me:

Whether we accomplish all of this or not depends on you.
I will be counting on you from the next world.
My dead eyes will be watching you from the tomb.
My last testament is only these three [few] words.
Sweetheart, keep this meaning in your heart.
Now please, you should go to a mighty fortress [safe place].
Although I am going to the land of death,
It will be beneficial to my mind if you survive.
If you accomplish the holy Dharma it will be of benefit to
both of us.
Before the arrival of the hail storm
It would be better to search quickly for a hiding place.

I make aspirations for your good health.
I make aspirations for your long life.
I make aspirations for your accomplishing the divine Dharma.
I make aspirations that you achieve your heart's wishes.
Now please stay well.

Having spoken, she suffocated. Then, Wide Wings,
tormented by the sorrow of the sharp thorns of suffering
suddenly driving into his heart, unable to respond, remained
and lamented: "Ah Kha Kha." At that time, from the midst
of the gale, hail pelted down. From the sky above, the
terrifying sound of thunder rumbled. The noose of lightning
flashed in the sky. Wide Wings was stunned, and squeezing
into a hole he continued lamenting: "Kye hud! Kye hud!"

Then the violent hail pelted down,
Landslides and floods seemed to fill the mountains and valleys.
Thunder and lightning seemed to fill the sky.
The crashing waves of all the rivers seemed to splash
toward the sky.

All of the mountains became barren.
All of the flooded fields became dried river beds.
All of the lakes turned red as blood.
All of the large flowers, bushes, and grasses were flattened.

The small ones were scattered.
The long ones were broken.
The short ones were pressed flat.
The little ones were destroyed without a trace.

After that, as the dark clouds cleared away and the bright
sun rose, Wide Wings went to the flower garden. All of
the large flowers growing in the swamps and the fields
had been flattened and scattered. The small ones had
disappeared without a trace. All of the lotuses in the water,
which were sunken into the depths when the hail fell upon
them, now floated above the water when the hail stopped.
The petals also opened and some bees pleasantly played and
flew among them. The flower in which Sweet Voice was
trapped had not been destroyed by the hail storm, but was
sunk in the depths of the water, and Sweet Voice was dead
by suffocation within it; her corpse stuck stiffly to the pistil.

Then Wide Wings' heart leapt to his throat, his eyes filled with
tears, and he was weighed by great sorrow. The brightness of
the sun, the blossoming of the flowers, the joyous play of the
other bees, and so forth, all of which previously had produced
joy in his mind, now became the source of more suffering. In a
feeble voice he uttered lamentations:

How sad, how sad, how sad.
What suffering, what suffering, what suffering.
Suffering, the nature of samsara, look at this, the miseries.
Impermanence, the city of illusion, look at this, the ruins.
Impermanence, the dwelling of illusion, look at this, how
it collapses.

Unreal, the deceptive objects of enjoyment, look at this,
how they change.

The flowers, well arranged in the past, their petals are
destroyed now.
The plants grown in the past are everywhere flattened now.
The valley of joy and happiness this morning
Has met with suffering now.
The body and mind of my excellent mate of the past have
separated now.

Wide Wings, cheerful in the past, has lost all hope now.
The objects of desire, attractive in the past,
Have become the source of suffering now.
The beautiful six-legged bee of this morning has become a
corpse now.

From thinking about these appearances:
Sad, sad, my mind is sad.
Confused, confused, my mind is confused.
Disturbed, disturbed, my mind is disturbed.
Trembling, trembling, my mind is trembling.

The sudden devil, the Lord of Death, arrived for her first.
When will he come for me?
O Lama, O Lama!
Sad Wide Wings is sad!

For turning my mind toward the Dharma,
Lama, please bestow blessings.

Then the golden bee's mind became very sad, and, unable
to stay, he went to the peak of the Lotus Mountain. He
flew among the turquoise junipers covered with dewdrops
near the residence of the Brahman boy, Lotus Joy [Patrul
Rinpoche], and sang a song of lamentation:

Alas, it is delightful, the garden of flowers,
It is depressing, the city of suffering.
They are attractive, the five objects of desire,
It is repelling, the suffering of the formations.
My life-long mate, my charming sweetheart,
Has turned into an ugly, rotten corpse.

Please heed me, please heed me, O Three Jewels, please heed me.
I remember, I remember, now I remember the holy Dharma.
Quickly, quickly I will enter the path of Dharma.

The following is a very famous saying in the Kadampa
tradition.

Since all that is constructed will fall down,
What is the use of houses?
Since all that is accumulated will dwindle,
What is the use of material wealth?
Since all who are assembled will separate,
What is the use of relatives and loved ones?
Since all who rise will fall,
What is the use of position?
Since all who are born will die,
What is the use of the appearances of this world?

It might not seem this way to us when we are not in the right
place or in the right state of mind because then we really want
to succeed in all of this. But if we are in the right place and
right mind, we will genuinely know this to be true, from the
very depth of our heart. Anyone who has been depressed in the
past probably has felt some of this.

My loving companion, bound to me by karma,
About now she will have arrived at the land of the
intermediate state.
At death, there is no hope other than the holy Dharma.

Since I have not practiced the beneficial holy Dharma myself,
Then even if I were rich, there would be nothing to be
bought with wealth,
Even if I had many allies, there would be nothing to be
taken by force,
Even if I were harmonious, there would be nothing with
which to ransom my friend.
Even if I had virtuous karma,
Virtuous karma could not be sent as a farewell gift.

The law of the Lord of Death cannot be put off.
Without practicing there is no benefit from studying.
Without plowing there is no benefit from a field.
Without riding there is no benefit from a horse.
Because I now realize the uselessness of everything,
I will devote the rest of my life to the holy Dharma.

I will not think about enemies, nor try to subdue them.
I will not think about relatives, nor try to serve them.
I will not think about wealth, nor have time to accumulate it.
I will not think about leaders, nor show deference toward them.

I will not think about friends, nor be attached with affection.
I will not think about clothing, nor will I have warm and
soft things.
I will not think about food, nor will I obtain tasty sweet food.
I will not think about houses, nor will I own dwellings.
I will not think about this life; the appearances of this
life are demonic.
I will not think about anything; delusory appearances are enemies.

I will remain in the state free from conceptions, in openness.
I will relax in the state of no-thought, in contemplation.
The Realized One, the one who has seen the
Dharmakaya in the state of non-meditation and
Sleeps at the foot of the mountain, is joyous.

Since delusory appearances are dissolved, there are few discursive thoughts.
Since acceptance and rejection are dissolved, there are no efforts at fabrication.
Since hope and fear are dissolved, free from wishes,
The Dissolved One who is free from delusions is joyous.

The unmodified mind as such, the ordinary mind,
Unmodified hair, the freely flowing locks,
Unmodified actions, aimless and spontaneous—one who is like this,
the Ascetic [Yogi] who has renounced artifice, is joyous.

Since his inner heat burns, he is carefree in nakedness.
Since he has perfected his meditation, he is delighted without food.
Since he has realized self-awareness, he is at ease in nakedness.
The Adept [Siddha] who has perfected the signs of the path is joyous.

Since he has great perseverance, he is comfortable with austerities.
Since he is able to observe his vows, he dwells by himself.
Sustained by drinking water and eating pebbles,
The Sage who accomplishes his esoteric training is joyful.

Whoever practices Dharma is joyful;
Whoever is attached to this life suffers.
Among the solitary mountains it is always joyous.
The city of samsara is suffering by all means.
Whoever relies on the Three Jewels is forever satisfied.
Whoever has hopes of profit and fame will always be impoverished.

I have paid and paid dues to my superior masters.
I am tired of paying them.
I will leave them to do what they like as they are.

I have given and given every gift to my inferior subordinates.
I am tired of giving to them.
I will leave them to do what they like.
I have protected and protected my mediocre relatives.
I am tired of protecting them.
I will leave them to do what they like.
I have fought and fought against my hateful enemies.
I am tired of fighting with them.
I will leave them to do what they like.
I have plowed and plowed my cultivated fields.
I am tired of plowing them.
I will leave them barren.
I have lived and lived in built-up fortresses.
I am tired of living in them.
I am going to leave for the solitary mountains.

I have eaten and eaten edible foods.
I am tired of eating.
I will enter into the ascetic life.
I have worn and worn wearable clothing.
I am tired of wearing them.
I will leap away in nakedness.
Now, I will practice and practice the practice of the very
holy Dharma!
Now, I will accomplish and accomplish the accomplishment
of the holy Dharma for death!
This is my vow. O Deities, please understand it!
This is my promise. My mind is the witness!

At that time, Lotus Joy thought: "Although the golden bee,
Wide Wings, was formerly sincere toward the Dharma,
reliable in all activities and good natured, at this time
the sudden revulsion arisen in him due to circumstantial
changes may not last a long time, so I must investigate it to
test him." So he said:

O heart-friend, golden bee, Wide Wings,
Why are you lamenting alone?
Today your lifelong friend assigned by karma
Has suddenly been caught in the noose of the Lord of Death.
However, don't feel sad but develop courage.
You should have the prosperity of worldly Dharma,
the foundation of the holy Dharma.
Worldly Dharma is the happiness and joy of samsara.

What follows sounds very familiar to me in some ways. Many
people have asked me questions like these.

What is the use of a Dharma that does not aspire to
happiness and joy?
The purpose of understanding Dharma is desire for
happiness and joy.

Even if one friend dies, how can you lack friends?
There is no example in the world of deprivation through the
death of a friend.
The rotation of happiness and suffering is the nature of samsara.
There will be hundreds of times when you think, "This is happiness."
The sudden renunciation of samsara is the display of Radzas
[a type of evil spirit].
It has no essence, don't you understand?

The sudden occurrences of faith are the changing shadows
of the mind.
They don't last, don't you understand?
Vain generosity is Alahasud [another type of evil spirit].
It is fruitless, don't you understand?
Unfortunate circumstances are sudden, adventitious, and momentary.
There is no poverty or prosperity to them, don't you understand?
The combination of the worldly and Dharma systems
is the thing to be accomplished by the wise ones.
In it is the path of liberation, don't you understand?

Transforming sensory objects into the path is the skillful
means of Tantra.
In it is the short path of liberation, don't you understand?

Holding the position of a king is an activity of the Bodhisattvas.
In it are the benefits for beings, don't you understand?
For people who accumulate wealth, it is possible to give.
In it is the completion of the six perfections, don't you understand?
Many promises without the mind's determination
Should be known as the cause of many transgressions in
the end.
Performing austerities without perseverance
Is the cause of the arising of wrong views in the end, so be careful!
Disgust and revulsion in samsara, which does not endure,
Is the cause of losing the provisions of this life in the end,
so be careful!

This means if you give to others with merely transitory
renunciation, you will find yourself in the end with nothing,
even though you desire to have a lot.

To stay in solitary mountains without having developed absorption
Is the cause of being fed up in the end, so be careful!
Without realizing the view, wandering in power [haunted] places
Is the cause of being possessed by gods and demons in the
end, so be careful!
Without the attainment of accomplishment, performing
esoteric activities
Is the cause of taking rebirth in hell in the end, so be careful!
Without changing one's own mind, to change costumes
Is the cause of others' feeling disgust for you in the end, so
be careful!
Without examination, having many sporadic ideas
Is the cause of developing regret in the end, so be careful!
Without certainty in a single activity, to be involved in
numerous activities

Is the cause of irritation of everyone in the end, so be careful!
Without obtaining the path of seeing, talking about foreknowledge
Is the cause of the impoverishment of self and others in the
end, so be careful!
Without having developed compassion, acting for beings
Is the cause of the arising of attachment in the end, so be careful!
Without making subtle investigations carefully,
It is not proper to say whatever thoughts come to mind and
It is not proper to do whatever one has said.

After catching, it is essential not to lose.
After holding, it is essential not to let go.
Having spoken, it is essential not to lie.

O golden bee, keep this in your mind.
It is the heart-advice of the relaxed Lotus Joy.
These are the experiences of my own mind, please don't
laugh at them.
These are loving confidences, please don't reprimand me.
Please keep it in mind and investigate it; it is the speech of truth.

Remember that he said all of those things to Wide Wings as a
test of his diligence and sincerity.

The golden bee, a little displeased in his mind, responded:

Ema, in the solitary forest
The Brahman boy is so relaxed.
Lotus Joy is charming.

To the tiny bee who is left alone,
Your consolation bespeaks your enduring friendship.
To Wide Wings who is lamenting,
Sharing confidential speech bespeaks your everlasting friendship.
To the golden bee who is tormented by sorrow,
Your giving consolation is a great kindness.

Your speech, which is harmonious with both systems,
worldly and spiritual,
If it really possesses excellent meaning, then it is wonderful.

In the nature of samsaric suffering,
I, the little bee who has developed revulsion,
Formerly stayed with a holy teacher,
Concentrated my mind on the holy Dharma, and
Drew the promise of practice in my heart.
It is not just a sudden reaction, I swear upon death.

I kept the solitary forests in my heart.
I maintained the lives of the earlier masters in my mind.
It is not just childish thoughts, I swear upon death.

I focused my mind on the Triple Gem.
I carried the gracious Lama on the crown in my head.
There is no error in the object of my focus, I swear upon death.

I maintained a broad mind toward hated enemies.
I kept an enduring friendship with my loving relatives.
I don't hate or fight, I swear upon death.

I made offerings to the Triple Gem.
I gave charity to the disabled.
I did not give or offer fruitlessly, I swear upon death.

I kept my qualities inside [hidden].
I unfurled others' qualities like banners.
I did not have pride or talk nonsense, I swear upon death.

The enduring, lifelong friend
Has suddenly been caught by the noose of the Lord of Death.
This time I saw the impermanence clearly and
Developed revulsion and renunciation.
In my talk there is no pretension, I swear upon death.

I have written the promises in the core of my heart.
I have whipped my practice with the whip of diligence.
In these words there are no lies, I swear upon death.
Affable Lotus Joy, have you met the teachers who are true
Buddhas, and
Do you possess the profound instructions?
Have you carried out the studies, impartially pondered
upon the scriptures, and
Have you dispelled the doubts about the words?
Have you observed your practices in solitary places, and
Have you developed uncontrived realization?
Have you sung joyful songs at the feet of rocky mountains, and
Has the power of meditative experiences blazed forth?
Have you performed your activities relaxedly and naturally, and
Attained the experience of equal taste as the path?
Have you seen the show of the cities of samsara, and
Developed revulsion from the depth of your heart?

Please give a speech in accordance with the Dharma.
Please sing a song in accordance with the path.
Please give an example that illustrates impermanence.
Please denounce the city of samsara.
Please speak of the virtues of the path of liberation.
Please speak the praises of the solitary mountains.

I, Wide Wings, the small golden bee,
Will make my residence in the solitary abodes.
I will maintain my affections toward the holy Dharma and friends.
I will watch the show of my own mind, and
I will have harmonious discussions with you.
I am presenting my words without any concealment.

Wide Wings wasn't very pleased with Lotus Joy's words. He
knew, on one hand, that Lotus Joy was trying to soothe him,
but on the other hand, he was not actually leading him in the
right way of the true path of the Dharma. However, Lotus

Joy was only giving Wide Wings the ideas that he could cope with—a mix of worldly life and Dharma together. Wide Wings' own personal experience had taught him how difficult this is to do since he'd failed in his resolve to do it in the past. In responding to Lotus Joy, he says that he truly wants to have the Dharma. He does not wish to be fooled by ideas or a mere conceptual realization of Dharma, only to be caught unprepared and not ready to truly let go.

> Then the Brahman boy, Lotus Joy, thought: "The golden bee, Wide Wings, has a good nature, enduring friendship, and stands straight. He is not like many other ordinary beings who possess vanity and many sporadic ideas. Nevertheless, if I guess from what he is saying now, it seems that he has faith in the Dharma from the depth of his heart. So, I should speak to him in accordance with what suits his mind."

We have to pay close attention to all of this—how sometimes we may possess a conceptual mind, an idealistic mind, and how it is not truly beneficial. At this point, Lotus Joy—Patrul Rinpoche—gives some very helpful advice.

> Kye Kye, harmonious heart-friend,
> You, Wide Wings, the golden bee!
> You entrusted your mind to the Triple Gem.
> You put your trust in the holy Dharma.
> You reduced the scope of your thoughts
> Through revulsion and renunciation, and
> You have devotion toward practice.
> These are the signs of having excellent aspirations in past lives.

Patrul Rinpoche is saying that if you have a saddened mind, *chyoshé* in Tibetan, the mind of renunciation, then you will make only short-term plans. By refraining from making long-term plans, you avoid all the hopes and fears in your mind. Since you never really know what's going to happen to you in the future anyway, making only short-term plans is practical.

It's important to develop the discipline of *dö chung chok shé,* which means "few desires, great contentment." This is a famous teaching in the Dzogpa Chenpo Longchen Nyingtik lineage from the great Omniscient Longchenpa. *Dö pa chung wa* means "diminished or little desire." *Chok shépa* means "feeling content with whatever we have." With the conviction that we really need nothing further, we no longer need to engage in planning our life for months or years to come. Cutting short such endless planning, we can commit to living completely in this moment, awake and fully alive, present with the realization that we need nothing more. Otherwise, we continue to be distracted by all our efforts to secure what is not securable—this unpredictable life. Cultivating contentment with what we have, without extravagance and greed, allows the peace of contentment to dawn in our heart.

> You have understood the constructed phenomena
> As impermanent and illusory apparitions.
> You have developed revulsion toward the city of samsara.
> You have avoided the evil minds of this life's eight worldly Dharmas.
> These are the signs that you have a karmic connection
> with the Dharma.
>
> Your analysis has opened toward the objects of studying
> and pondering.
> You have understood the acceptances and rejections
> of the profound causation [karma].
> You know the activities of the Holy Sons of the Victors.
> You have found the entrance to the excellent path.
> These are the signs that you are accepted by a holy Lord.

To the fortunate little bee,
I, a disciple of an excellent Lama,
Give the introduction of the excellent certainty.
Accept it as an addition to your excellent intentions.

In the city of an inferior samsara,
The container [world] is called Maya, the illusory appearances.
The contained [beings] are called solid delusions.
The container and contained are gathered together
By frantically being involved in evil deeds.
Suffering is spread just as a fire spreads in the forest.

By having turned one's back on virtuous deeds,
Happiness and joy become like the stars of dawn.
By having embraced evil activities,
The age of dregs[3] draws near as the evening shadows of
the mountains.
Within the grinder of the cruel hatred
Is marked the navel hole of desire.
In it is poured the popped barley of the humans of the
upper realms.
Having been ground, it falls out in the depths of the
inferior realms.

Watch the process of a few big grains at the top of the grinder.
Watch the process of the increase into many fine particles
of flour at the bottom.
See the manner of how subtle the process of cause and
result is!

In ancient times, in the Jambu continent of the human realm,
The towns were joined together breadthwise and lengthwise.
Roosters could travel from house to house by flying.
Wealth and happiness could compete with that of the gods.
The leaders were the Universal Kings.

They ruled their states by the power of their golden wheels.
The subjects were contained within the four continents and
eight subcontinents.
The law was the ten virtuous deeds.
Human beings increased and migrated to the upper realms
of the gods.
The gods increased and filled the flower gardens.

He is referring to how, in ancient times, there were many
virtuous kings that led the people into virtuous acts, and
therefore many people were reborn in the heavenly realms.

Nowadays, in the age of dregs,
The cities are lined-up broken walls.
The barren fields stretch out in chains.
The people eat meat and blood for enjoyment.
The leaders are the messengers of hell.
They rule their states by the power of war and death.

Here, he is saying that leaders now are messengers for hell—
like demonic butlers, they lead you straight to the hell realms.
He is criticizing all degenerate people.

The subjects are wandering beings with evil karma.
The laws are based upon the means to get food and the
spread of deception.
The endless roots of society are controlled by robbers.
The robbers are heading for the gates of the city of hell.
Their progress is the increase of the heat and cold of hell.
Their war is the victory of the demigods and Raksasas.
Their consumption is the development of sickness and plague.
The rulers, on their seats of power, defraud their subjects.
Through cunning they punish innocent people.
Through lies they enumerate the faults of their workers.
Through deceit they throw themselves and others into destitution.

These were also degenerate times for many people because of their negative actions, which commonly lead to rebirth in the lower realms.

> The spiritual masters underneath their parasols deceive their disciples.
> They employ the holy Dharma as a shield.
> They roar their lies of foreknowledge with random guesses.
> They perform empowerment as a business to accumulate wealth.
> They pay attention to the dispositions of the worldly leaders.
> For Dharma practice they perform ceremonies only to repulse the unfavorable circumstances of the townspeople.

This refers to the lamas, or maybe even me. It means that some things a lama may do, or that people see the lama do, only pretend to be like Dharma. Actually, it's turning Dharma-less behavior into the appearance of Dharma.

> The great meditators in their hermitages deceive their devotees.
> In their hermitages they sleep like corpses.
> If lay people see them, they straighten their bodily postures.
> If they have wealth, they keep it hidden somewhere else.
> To their patrons they express flattery.

> The lay people deceive themselves.
> Their minds are like a potter's wheel.
> They look at what they want and then turn the wheel accordingly.
> Their words are like the tools of a smith.
> They are examined for their suitability and then altered accordingly.
> Their activities are like the sky in the spring,
> Now it is clear, now it is dark.
> Lasting relationships are like the suckers of bees,
> They are there while they suck, but absent when finished.
> Flattering behavior is like a drawing of a thangka,
> It is beautiful in front, but there is nothing behind it.

> Affections are like a dish of lung.
> There is something in the mouth, but nothing
> substantial [satisfying].

Some people are able to sense what it is you would like to hear, so they try to please you and manipulate you into liking them and doing things for them. This eventually turns them into *your* boss. In the end, they get what they want from you by using their persuasive power and manipulating you to serve their needs. Their appreciation for you is always stated as, "Oh, I really appreciate you. I really like you. I really admire you." But it's like a one-dimensional picture—beautiful in the front, but in the back, it's blank. Like that, they flatter you with words and gestures, but they're not really sincere. This is very important for all of us to contemplate—especially any ladies who might be susceptible if they like hearing pleasing things about themselves—because men can be very tricky. Such flattery and affection are as insubstantial as cotton candy that immediately dissolves in your mouth. I urge you to really examine this, again and again.

> Religious people deceive others.
> Their study and pondering is like the body of a tadpole;
> The head is big but the tail is thin.
> Their perseverance is like the mouth of a frog.
> It is there when they hear but not when they practice.
> They deceive their teachers with lies.
> With cunning they craft the unspiritual into the spiritual.
> With deceit they gossip about the practice of meditation.

The comparison of deceitful religious people to frogs is apt: the tadpole's head is quite big, and then the body thins out. Although small, frogs make huge sounds from deep in their bellies. We understand this—right? When you are just beginning to practice, you practice quite consistently, and then later, you practice less. Then as you move further along, you practice even less. You can really see this in the practice schedules that people record—how people are not consistent in their practice discipline over time.

When the earth is captured by robbers,
How can the highways of truth be maintained?
When the country is filled with fools,
To whom will the scriptures of the wise ones be taught?
When the rulers destroy their own laws,
In whom can the subjects depend through their happiness
and sorrow?
When the spiritual teachers are only concerned for their
own needs,
Who will work for the benefit of the weak?
When the leaders are robbing their servants and retinues,
Who will take care of the destitute?

Alas, alas, alas!
In me, the young boy, revulsion has developed from the
depth of my heart.
Between the teeth of the Raksasas of impermanence,
The beings of the three realms are wandering.

Like the small insects that get sucked into a lizard's mouth, those insects may have felt they had time left. Similarly, even though your life is nearly "in the lizard's mouth," you may still feel like you have a lot of time.

Still bound by the attachment of apprehending
phenomena as permanent,
Having worked and worked for their necessities in this life,
At the time of death they will struggle,
Grasping their hands to their chests because of remorse.

I don't know whether this happens so often in the West, but in the Tibetan culture, people who have accumulated a lot of negative deeds in their life, like hunters, will experience hallucinations of animals chasing and attacking them. They will beat their chests because they know what they've done and deeply regret it on their deathbed.

They make sure to fulfill tomorrow's needs,
But they postpone the Dharma for the next life.
Look at how the bodies that were alive this morning
This evening are cold corpses.
Either tomorrow or the next life, do you know which will come first?

What is a beautiful body this morning could be a corpse by this evening. For instance, you could be driving this morning, have a fatal accident, and by evening, your body is a corpse. The question is, which will it be—tomorrow or the next life?

I, the young boy, Lotus Joy,
Met the Lama, the real Buddha,
Who accepted me with a gracious mind.
My faith, devotion, and trust are one-pointed.
My devotion never wavered.
I said whatever arose in my mind.
I never made a choice about the terms that I used.
My activities are natural and spontaneous.
I have never deceived others nor am I two-tongued.
I have trust in one person and one deity.
I never sought refuge from others.
I spent a long time near holy teachers.
The number of the wise teachers I have had is many.
My impartial study of scriptures is vast.
Therefore I know what is Dharma and what just looks like Dharma.

Little golden bee, Wide Wings,
If you want to practice the Dharma from the heart, and

If you have developed revulsion from the depth of your mind
You need certain teachings in order to reject various experiences.
At the beginning, when you seek the path of Dharma,
There are experiences that are similar to revulsion.
First is the revulsion caused by the languishing of a
suffering person.
Second is adventitious circumstances.
Third is the abuse of lovers.
Fourth is the exhausting hardship of work.
Fifth is the interaction of elements in the body.
These are similar to revulsion but are not revulsion.

There are experiences that are similar to renunciation.
First is the renunciation caused by the desire for
attractiveness by changing costumes.
Second is desiring relaxation in the comfort of a hermitage.
Third is to perform recitations with the hope of achieving
esoteric powers.
Fourth is to make pilgrimages to see the world.
Fifth is the desire for the eight worldly dharmas[4] that create
hope and fear.
These are similar to renunciation but are not renunciation.

He's talking about two kinds of renunciation here. One happens
when you're just fed up with your life, so you want to renounce it.
Another is *truly* seeing samsara as suffering, and then becoming
genuinely inspired by that to practice the Dharma.

There are ways of life that are similar to living in a hermitage.
First is to be strict outside and loose inside.
Second is to have no schedule and to be careless.
Third is to be involved in physical skills and sciences.
Fourth is to indulge in sudden works and activities.
Fifth is to waste the human life in sleep.
Even if you live in hermitages there is no essence.

There are experiences that are similar to disgust with samsara.
First is the counseling of someone who cannot succeed in worldly dharmas.
Second is the sporadic speech of wild, crazy people who run around.
Third is the loud boasting of thoughtless people.
Fourth is the lack of concern for wealth of apathetic people.
Fifth is the sudden destitution of people who lack ideas for recovery.
These are similar to disgust with samsara but are not disgust.

He's saying that somebody with a heavy, pessimistic mind sometimes gets fed up with their life, and they want to renounce everything, but it's just their heavy and pessimistic state of mind that's motivating them—not a true understanding of the Dharma or of pervasive suffering, along with the genuine motivation for liberation. Some days are challenging due to passing circumstances. Negative circumstances can arise that create a sense of hopelessness and a state of mind that is unable to accomplish anything beneficial.

There are ways that are similar to wandering with renunciation in the world.
First is the way of those wishing to be excited by seeing sights.
Second is the way of those going to see pilgrimage places having no faith.
Third is the way of those doing circumambulations without knowing the benefits.
Fourth is the way of robbers who pick on others intending to rob them.
Fifth is the way of those rushing around without any thoughts.
These are similar to pilgrimage but are not pilgrimage.

There are ways that are similar to retreat.
First is performing recitations without visualizing the forms of deities.

Second is practicing the developmental and perfecting
stages without certainty.
Third is doing wrathful practices wishing to attain power.
Fourth is completing the sessions of counting the numbers
of recitations.
Fifth is practicing the four activities for the hopes of this life.
These are similar to retreat but have no essence.

Then, when you pursue the practice of Dharma,
There are practices that are similar to going for refuge.
First is the enumeration of the accumulation of words.
Second is not knowing how to rely on the Triple Gem with
a trusting mind.
Third is not knowing the special distinctions of the objects
of refuge.
Fourth is not knowing the virtues of the Triple Gem.
Fifth is going for refuge with expectations.
These are similar to going for refuge, but they have no essence.

There are practices that are similar to developing
the mind of enlightenment [Bodhicitta].
First is the development of the mind of enlightenment,
desiring good for oneself.
Second is expecting to have results and maturation.
Third is compassion with partiality.
Fourth is the development of the mind of enlightenment verbally.
Fifth is not to know, except for hearsay, about the
disciplines of training.
Even though these are called the development of
the mind of enlightenment, there is no essence.

There are practices that are similar to the developmental
stage [bsKyed-Rim].
First is the pride of being the deity without clarity of the
visualized form.
Second is the clarity of visualization without the pride.

89

Third is the doubts and hopes of the apprehending mind.
Fourth is the wrathfulness without the mind of
enlightenment [Bodhicitta].
Fifth is the lacking of the applications of purification,
perfection, and maturation.
Although it is called the development stage, it is the cause
of samsara.

There are practices that are similar to the perfection stage
[rDzogs-Rim].
First is practice on the channels and energy
without knowing luminous absorption [A'od-gSal].
Second is practice on dreams without perfecting them into
illusions [sGyu-Ma'i].
Third is practice on the path of skillful means
without liberating the knots of the channels.
Fourth is practice on the Great Seal [Phyag-Ch'en] and
Great Perfection [rDzogs-Pa Ch'en-Po]
without knowing the method of liberation.
Fifth is practice of Direct Approach [Thod-rGal] with
attachment to the visions.
These are called great perfections, but there is no essence.

Lastly, when you attain the results of the practice,
There are results that are similar to acting for the benefit of others.
First is having foreknowledge of the appearance of
meditative experiences.
Second is having certain accomplishments due to
possession by gods and demons.
Third is giving teachings that accumulate the eight
worldly dharmas.
Fourth is gathering retinues without leading them to Dharma.
Fifth is giving instructions, but having no experiences.
These are similar to the action of benefiting others but
have no essence.

I think it's very important for all of us to remember these fifty-five points.

These fifty-five comparisons are not given as a mirror for looking at others' faults.
This is even refreshing for myself.
You should also keep it always in your mind.
When you practice Dharma just in appearance,
As to whether various kinds of deviations arise or not,
It is necessary to exert yourself in precise examination and correction.

Though my words have no great beauty,
The meaning possesses the taste and sustenance of nine innumerable profundities.
It is the oral transmission of the peerless Lama.
If you intend to practice the holy Dharma from the heart,
There is no need for gossip and boasting,
There is no need to prepare a show of provisions,
There is no need to fix a time,
There is no need to go away and seek Dharma.

The holy Dharma is like the body and its limbs.
Whenever you need it, it is within yourself.
Every instant you should exert yourself.
At all times you should clearly remind yourself.
In each moment you should correct yourself.
Every day you should reprimand yourself for your evil deeds.
Every morning you should make vows.
In every period of meditation you should analyze yourself.
Even incidentally, you should not separate yourself from Dharma.
In the stream of time you should not forget the Dharma.

If the practice is not performed in its subtlety,
Then for the practitioner who puts on a great show of practicing Dharma
It has no way of becoming a true form of Dharma.

First, carried off by laziness in the mountains;
Second, practicing in the monasteries with distractions;
Third, seeking solitude and desiring comforts;
In the world there is nothing worse than these three.
Divine Prince, do you follow?

Happiness is not good, suffering is good.
If you are happy, the five poisonous emotions rage.
If you suffer, previously accumulated evil deeds are exhausted.
Suffering is the kindness of the Lama.

Praise is not good, blame is good.
If praised, then pride and arrogance increase.
If blamed, then one's own faults are exposed.
Defamation is the gift of the gods.

High position is not good, a low position is good.
If you are high, pride and jealousy arise.
If you are low, openness and dedication increase.
A low position is the seat of superior ones.

Wealth is not good, poverty is good.
If you are wealthy, there is the great suffering of collecting
and protecting.
If you are poor, austerity and the holy Dharma
are accomplished.
The body [life] of a beggar is the goal of the religious person.

Being given to is not good, being stolen from is good.
If one is given to, then the load of karmic debt increases.
If one is stolen from, then the debts of future lives are paid back.
Contentment is the crown jewels [common wealth] of the
Noble Ones.

Friends are not good, enemies are good.
Friends hinder the path of liberation.

Enemies are the objects of patience.
The practice of equal taste is the crucial juncture.

If you want to practice according to Dharma, you should
act according to this advice.
If you want to make up your mind, you should
act according to this advice.
If you want to live in a solitary retreat, you should
act according to this advice.
If you want to roam around the world, you should
act according to this advice.
The six condensed points, the essential profound advice,
is the oral transmission of the sole father Guru.
These six words are the essence of the heart.
Except to you, my sole friend, I have not shown even a
hint to others.

Ema, golden bee, divine prince!

For the sacred pilgrimage place to stay in, there is the high-
peaked Lotus Mountain.
This is the pure land of the sole deity, Tara.
This is the palace of Avalokiteshvara.[5]
This is the place of accomplishment of the Lotus King.
Look at this mountain, the body of the Noble One.
It possesses his complete form, relaxing in the natural
state of mind.
Look at the rocks, the speech of the Noble One.
There are countless self-emerged six-syllable mantras.
Look at the trees, the blue-green groves.
They perfect the characteristics of the Land of
Turquoise Leaves, the Pure Land of Tara.
This land is surrounded by vicious, venomous snakes.
It is difficult for small-minded, ill-fortuned people to
cross into it.

It possesses the characteristics of the Potala Mountain,
the Pure Land of Avalokiteshvara.
In front is the heart emanation—the Lotus Born,
Sending forth emanations for the sake of beings.
Nearby is the beautiful palace of the women saints.
The time for these goddesses to serve beings has arrived.
In the heart of Avalokiteshvara is the meditation cave of
me, Lotus Joy.

For the deity, we will accept the powerful Avalokiteshvara.
For the mantra, we will recite the six syllables.
For the Dharma, we will meditate on loving-kindness
and compassion.
For the path, we will pursue the blissful path of the Sons of
the Victors.
Then, even if we should desire suffering, we will experience
only happiness!
Happiness for this life, joy for the next life—A-la-la
[wonderful]!
We will proceed from happiness to happiness.
Eternal happiness will never change, A-la-la!
Let us make prayers to the Lord Lama.
His compassion will not fail, A-la-la!

Let us beseech Avalokiteshvara as our tutelary deity.
The accomplishments will not be postponed, A-la-la!
It is a great wonder!
Don't you think this is a great wonder, Divine Prince?

This is Patrul Rinpoche describing his own experience. He
says that even if he desires unhappiness, he only experiences
happiness. When you have turned unhappiness into happiness,
then how could you not always experience happiness?

First, my heart vows;
Second, your heart wishes;

If they agree, then we will be able to follow after the lives of
the past masters.
Let us renounce the path of the eight worldly dharmas like
stones on the road,
Abandon the appearances of this life like harmful poison,
And practice subtly on diligence.
Let the instructions strike our own faults,
Let us throw boasting and gossiping to the wind.
Let us maintain our attitude along the path of Bodhicitta.
If we agree on these, then we have established the basis
for counsel.
Two brotherly friends who have agreed in harmony
Proceed together along the path of liberation.
We are protected by these aspirations.
Throughout all successive lives we will meet together.
We will practice the Bodhisattva activities together.
Do you think this is proper, Divine Prince?
This is the condensation of the meanings, A-la-la!
This is the joining together of all the essential instructions.

When this had been said, Wide Wings agreed very much,
and his wisdom was perfected.

As the moon waxes in the night sky of autumn,
The divine Manjushri displays the signs and characteristics
of youth.
For the Buddhas, he is the wisdom-being.
For all beings, he is the ultimate nature of their minds.

For the realm of endless beings, the characteristic of which
is suffering,
The One with Unblinking Eyes [Avalokiteshvara]
stretches his long arms of loving-kindness.
For the Buddhas, he is the great compassion.
For all beings, he is their seed of liberation.

The holder of the profound treasure of mystery
Is the Holder of the Vajra [Vajrapani], the master
of the mysteries of all the Buddhas.
For the Buddhas, he is their wisdom-actions.
For the realm of beings, he is the presence of the union
of naked intrinsic awareness and emptiness.

I pray to the Sons of the Victors, the Lords of the Three Classes.
Lord Lama, who is inseparable from them, please bestow
your blessings.
Until the attainment of enlightenment I hold you as
the family Lord without separation.
O Compassionate Ones, please hold me continually
with compassion.

This speech, which is in accordance with the divine
doctrine, known as the Dramatic Performance in the Lotus
Garden, at the request of the boy Trashi Geleg, with his
root points, is written by the relaxed Patrul.

This is the conclusion of *Holy Dharma Advice, A Drama in
the Lotus Garden*. Although this translation is not as poetic in
English as it is in the original Tibetan, I think the meaning

still comes through quite well. If you could contemplate the story repeatedly, that would be helpful. Digest these teachings, contemplate them, and sit with them.

Part I: Notes

1   The law of the cause and effect of actions—that every action one performs has a commensurate effect in this and future lives.

2   A vocative exclamation.

3   Tib.: *sNyigs-Ma*. This age has five characteristics indicating degeneration: short life span, emotional struggles, perverted views, sentient beings difficult to tame, and declining prosperity.

4   These are eight kinds of worldly attitudes. They are: wanting to have gain, fame, praise, and happiness, and wanting not to have loss, infamy, blame, or suffering.

5   Avalokiteshvara is the embodiment of the compassion of the buddhas who manifests in the form of a bodhisattva.

Part II:

Translation by Dzigar Kongtrul Rinpoche
and Elizabeth Mattis Namgyel
with 1990 Commentary

Part II: Overview

The Drama of the Flower-Gathering Garden is a poetic narrative written by the renowned Patrul Rinpoche, who was born in the early part of the nineteenth century. He was a student of Jigme Gyalwe Nyugu, one of the chief disciples of the great master of the Nyingmapa school, Rigdzin Jigme Lingpa. Patrul Rinpoche was considered an incarnation of the Indian pandit Shantideva, author of the *Bodhicaryavatara*, and was famous throughout his lifetime as a sage, teacher, writer, and poet.

Unlike most teachers of his caliber, Patrul Rinpoche did not gather assemblages of monks and students around him, nor did he build any monasteries. Instead, he taught as he wandered from place to place and never accumulated personal possessions or put on an outward show. His great interest was in the harmonious blending of the tightly logical Buddhist philosophy with the nonconceptual practice of meditation. To this end he was active in propagating a completely nonsectarian approach to the Buddhadharma, which came to flower in the late 19th century in Eastern Tibet as the Rimé movement. Patrul Rinpoche was the author of a great number of texts encompassing all aspects of the Buddha's teachings, and his work is held in highest esteem for its profundity, precision, beauty, and pithiness. This text, *The Drama of the Flower-Gathering Garden*, is no exception.

The location of this story, the Flower-Gathering Garden itself, is an actual place in the small Buddhist kingdom of Derge in Eastern Tibet. Derge is famous for its devotion to the Buddha's teachings and for the elaborate library of Buddhist texts, printed from wood blocks, which are housed there. It is said that one of the first kings of Derge, Chogyal Tenpa Tsering, commissioned wood blocks for the printing of 108 volumes of the Buddha's teachings. To ensure that the carving was deep and clear, the king paid the carver with the amount of gold dust that could be contained within the incised blocks.

Patrul Rinpoche often practiced near this kingdom in a place that was sacred to Padmasambhava, the great Indian guru who brought Buddhism to Tibet in the 9th century. Also nearby was the Flower-Gathering Garden, where this story takes place. It's based on the true story of Tashi Gelek, who was a high official in the Derge Court. He and his wife led a luxurious life, and like most upper-class people, they were knowledgeable about the Buddha's teachings. Though they were drawn to practice the Buddhist teachings, since they were very busy with their lives, they had little time to do so. When Tashi Gelek's wife contracted smallpox, to prevent further spread of the infection, she was quarantined in a cave. As she was dying there, she described her feelings to her mate and exhorted him to practice the teachings in earnest. After her death, Tashi Gelek renounced his worldly life and became a close disciple of Patrul Rinpoche.

Patrul Rinpoche recounts their story as the story of two bees. The male bee's body is yellowish, so I often refer to him as "Golden Bee," but his name is Dabyang. The female bee is turquoise, and her name is Ngakyen, which means "beautiful voice." Dabyang means "far-reaching wings" or "talented wings." The two bees, Ngakyen and Dabyang, are very bright and wealthy. Though they received teachings on the four noble truths, they don't do any serious practice but remain involved in their worldly life.

One day, the female bee is enjoying the nectar on a flower while the male bee is flying around enjoying the scenery. Suddenly, a black cloud covers the earth and causes all the flowers to close. The female bee is caught inside a flower, and the male bee is outside. This is a very dramatic, emotional experience, and in the end, it hails; the flowers are cut down and destroyed, and the female bee is suffocating in the flower. Outside, the male bee is desolate, and he sings songs of his sorrow.

Then the male bee visits several powerful animals who seem to know what they're doing. They say they can help the situation, but nothing they do turns out absolutely right. Finally, the male bee turns aside from this spiritual materialism. In the story, the animals represent spirits of beings and spiritual teachers. After his mate dies, the male bee meets Patrul Rinpoche, receives teachings, and goes on to practice. So, this is the story of how intelligent, well-favored, well-meaning people—despite their advantages—still get caught up in the world of pleasure and pain, and how one of them suffered and died, and the other suffered and entered the path of liberation.

This story touches me deeply because of how well it addresses our present situation. We have a lot of material pleasures and preoccupations, and we think we have plenty of time. Thus, I think this story is one of the most effective teachings to open one's ignorance and see how much our lives are involved in fakery and the subtler materialism often concealed in spiritual pursuits. The story also contains a complete summary of the path of liberation—from finding a teacher and taking refuge, through developing bodhicitta, Vajrasattva, mandala offering, chöd, and guru yoga. Everything is here. I have really gotten a lot out of this story myself, and I hope this will be true for anyone who reads it.

Part II: Text & Commentary

Part One
OM VAJRA TIK SHANA

The essence of prosperity is the essence of the glorious sound: that which is the sound of the Dharma teachings. By writing this story, I plant the flag of the Dharma firmly into the ground. Bless me, Manjushri, so that the teachings flourish and are accomplished without obstacle.

At one time, on a very broad, high-peaked mountain, quilted with forest and inhabited by the flower yogini, Tara herself, the Master of the Flower, King of the Lotus, showered his blessings and planted his footprint. In this mountain was a cave in the shape of a half-moon. The inhabitant of this cave was the yogi, Pema Jyipa, who came from the plateau of flowers. He was the knower of all things, the goer to all places, the resident of all dwellings; he was compatible with all beings. He practiced the bodhisattva's path, the path of faultless conduct,

which is the practice of the flower. And like a lotus floating on the water of essence-mind, he meditated on nonattachment.

Not so far away from this was a place called the Flower-Gathering Garden. It was surrounded by trees and blankets of high green grass and flowers with many different qualities. Some flowers were long-stemmed, some in full bloom, some heavy and bending with nectar. There were young stems brilliant in color; those not yet ripened; tightly-closed flowers that had reached maturation with less pollen; those dry of nectar; and those darkened, withered, or without petals. Those that were proud and voluptuous strutted their stamens, while others remained below. Some were mere seedlings reaching up to the sun. Each flower had at least one of these qualities in the Flower-Gathering Garden.

In this garden, many groups of bees circled through the air. One bee in particular was golden and named Dabyang, which means "far-reaching wings." There was another small turquoise bee named Ngakyen, which means "beautiful voice." These two bees were mates, and they remained among the flowers and other bees in the Flower-Gathering Garden. Dabyang, the golden bee, was young, strong, and alert, with a bright intelligence and an open heart. He had little desire to chase after new friends. His personality was calm, and he enjoyed being generous. Ngakyen, the turquoise bee, also had courage and natural openness, which is characteristic of all generous beings, and she had a desire to help others. Her personality was also very smooth. She had a natural interest in the Dharma, an honest character, and a mind with little jealousy and possessiveness.

Between these two bees there was much affection, smiling, and loving speech. With compatibility and good conduct, they spent their lives together and secretly sang to each other beautiful songs, such as this one sung by Ngakyen:

Kyé, kyé—this youthful body is a magical display,
A most beautiful painting existing
without the stroke of an artist's brush.

This cornucopia of brilliant flowers
and sweet nectar naturally arises.
Without the intention of collecting it,
it exists by the power of karma.
The petals of these flowers are like silky cushions.
Without the skill of a weaver's hand,
they exist naturally for your comfort.
This golden pollen, so sweet and delectable,
can be found within the flower.
Without being created, it is the most delicious drink of amrita.
Comfort and happiness appear as a result of previous merit;
without fabrication they arise.
Cultivating our mind with the Dharma, our bodies become precious.
It is unnecessary to praise and envy the two-legged beings
who use their speech and reason
for trivial or mean-spirited activities.

Kyé, kyé—listen, my dear heart.
Here in the Flower-Gathering Garden, there is much beauty.
Sweet, nutritious nectar is plentiful.
Beings of our same speech are abundant.
But this wealth is as ethereal as a summer cloud.
Circumstances of death are many and unexpected.
Happiness and sadness change moment by moment.
The host of death comes closer and closer.
Spending one's life desiring happiness and pleasure
is a meaningless and temporary diversion.
It is possible to keep oneself busy and
distracted with mundane tasks for a lifetime.

What's the use of this type of living?
The garden is so beautiful and serene; nevertheless,
bid farewell to it at death. It has no ultimate benefit.
With this understanding in mind, let us practice the Dharma.
My dear friend, do you feel this way, too?

When Ngakyen finished this song, Dabyang replied,

Lek so, lek so, my dear heart. You are so right! So true; so true!
Your heartfelt song, melting into the heart,
becomes deathless amrita.
The Flower-Gathering Garden becomes
comparable to the god realm itself!
We who share the fortunate wealth and great
pleasures of this place are experiencing the
fruit of our previous generosity.

But however beautiful this place is,
it has the impermanent nature of samsara.
Though it is rich with flowers and nectar,
like the wealth of a magician, it has no solidity.
Samsara is a place of no essence.
As you have such strong determination,
I will also take these ideas to heart.

What will change when we decide to practice?
My dear companion, let us follow the path of Dharma.

There is no essence in cultivated wealth.
Though you try with effort to collect it,
it always becomes another's.
Even well-looked-after servants have no ultimate benefit.
With good intention, you look after them,
but you end up with yet another enemy.
A well-built house may seem to protect you,
but it may end up being the cause of your death.
A well-cultivated field, however beneficial we view it,
is really a slaughterhouse for insects.

Let us follow the path with great thought and an even mind.
A confident decision and determination lead to success!

Commentary on Part One

In this rocky mountain was a cave the shape of a half-moon where Patrul Rinpoche did many years of retreat. There, it is said, he followed the way of a bodhisattva—putting the benefits of others ahead of oneself—which is called in the poem "the practice of the flower." He meditated on nonattachment "like a lotus floating on the water of essence-mind," which means meditating on emptiness and not being drowned by a self-important, egotistical mind. Realizing that attachment is inherently empty is understanding the true nature of mind. At that point, true nature and essence are the same. The idea behind the practice of the flower is that bodhisattvas are born into samsara but are not drowned in it because of their realization of emptiness nature, just like the lotus—born in water but not drowned by it.

Samsara is a place of no essence and means "cycle of suffering." For example, if a bee were caught in a bottle, the bee would spiral in the bottle with no means of escape. Similarly, samsara is a cycle of endless suffering. One has the ability through positive deeds to go to the higher realms, and conversely, through negative deeds, one will go to the lower realms. However, one cannot be free from that cycle until attaining liberation.

Near the place where Pema Jyipa practiced in this way is a beautiful garden, a kind of paradise where all the riches of the plant world are freely displayed. Living there in great delight, enjoying this garden, are the two bees. They not only have the great happiness of living there, but their happiness is multiplied by having someone to share it with. They pass their time together cheerfully, complimenting one another and exchanging intimacies in low voices that others cannot hear. They often sing songs in appreciation of one another and their unfettered life in the garden.

The turquoise bee, Ngakyen, sings to Dabyang, the golden bee, about his beauty and how delightful it is to share in these wonderful surroundings. She says that if they turn their minds toward the Dharma, they could have no higher birth. Their existence resembles the realm of the gods, which is ideally pleasurable and delightful—so much so that it is difficult to overcome attachment to it. Even though at the end of a very long cycle of time the god realm also disintegrates, to the sudden horror and shock of its occupants, the bliss of such a realm is so perfect and prolonged that it is almost impossible to realize the truth of impermanence, much less to do anything about it when the sudden change comes.

In the human realm, it is much easier to realize the three marks of existence. These three marks are: impermanence, dissatisfaction, and the absence of anything that can be pointed to as a self. In some realms, such as those of the gods and demi-gods, these truths only become evident when it is too late. In others, such as the various forms of the hell realm or the animal realm, the suffering and fear are so powerful that any clarity of mind is difficult to attain. Within the human realm itself, we have approximations of these states, such as in the seemingly glamorous lives of people who are inconceivably rich or powerful, or those whose poverty and degradation are almost unimaginably intense. Nonetheless, in general, it is in the human realm where there is some balance between pleasure and pain so that one can see the truth about existence and do something to liberate oneself from its endless recycling of pain, pleasure, and delusion. Cultivating our minds with the Dharma, our bodies become precious.

So, Ngakyen sings a song in which she celebrates their life together, but at the same time she knows that it will not last. She says that to make the greatest use of their opportunity that combines the advantages of the god realm with that of the human, they should seek out and practice the Dharma to attain liberation.

Dabyang replies that Ngakyen's words have melted into his heart like amrita, the nectar of true bliss that is beyond death. In other words, her song melts into his heart and makes it unchangeable. He agrees that they must find a teacher to guide them. He also emphasizes the importance of approaching the Dharma with a calm and steady mind. If one approaches the Dharma with excitement, when that excitement dissipates, one's original intention will not be realized. Really take these thoughts to heart; write them on your heart like someone carving on stone. Since we alone can control our own minds, it is up to us to seal our conviction.

Dabyang and Ngakyen are quite amazing. Usually we only look into our circumstances with any degree of sharpness when things are not going well for us. But here, two beings who are in a very good state somehow have the sensitivity and courage to try to look at things clearly and to form some resolve to go further than their delightful way of life. It is very much to their credit that they do so.

Part Two

At this time, quite close to the Flower-Gathering Garden, dwelt one sage, Dhunkun Drubpa, whose name means "All-Fulfilling Wish." He had a great, kind mind, gentle manner, and especially enjoyed benefiting beings. The two bees went to see him and prostrated to him, making great offerings of honey. They enjoyed beautiful conversation with the sage, which led to a request for teachings.

> Kyé, kyé, great yogi! You are truly the vision of the Buddha.
> Please give us teachings of the Buddha.
> You are the lamp of the Dharma.
> Give us some essential teachings.
> You are the perfect image of the noble Sangha.
> Teach us the conduct of the sons and daughters of
> the Victorious Ones.
> Accept us as followers of your noble being.

The sage was delighted at this request and cleared his voice. This is what he said:

NAMO ARAYA TAMPA
I prostrate to those Enlightened Ones
who have conquered all the kleshas.
To the great freer of beings, the Lord of the Lords,
incomparable son of the Shakya, I prostrate.
Please turn the minds of the six realms toward the Dharma.

Dabyang and Ngakyen, listen carefully to this:

The words of Lord Buddha will be in the palm of your hand.
This is the essence-nectar of the Dharma,
so keep this in your heart.

É MA! The beings of the six realms
have been dwelling in samsara for eternity.
Karma, kleshas, and delusions are never-ending.
There are periods of time for billions of eons that it is rare
for any being to hear the name of the Three Jewels.
So, to meet the Buddhadharma is like seeing a star
in the daytime.
And this time, the fourth leader of sentient beings into liberation,
son of the Se Tsang [Shakya], incomparable Buddha,
has come into this world
and turned the Wheel of the Dharma three times!
In the five-hundred-and-tenth time,
the fourth Buddhadharma will have ceased.
But as this time has not yet come,
we have the chance to follow the path.
Special circumstances allow us a connection with a noble teacher.
Unless one follows the path whole-heartedly,
a fortunate rebirth will be difficult to attain.
Just hearing the name of the Three Jewels will be difficult.

É MA! Deluded, suffering, samsaric beings grasp at composite,
impermanent things as if they were everlasting.
Even the five outer environmental elements are temporary.

The sentient beings who live in these elements
inevitably diminish.
Meanwhile, the four seasons change.
Look at the Victorious Ones and their sons and daughters
who are subject to impermanence and death.
Universally powerful Brahma and Vishnu will also find
the Lord of Death's noose around their necks.

Who knows where and when one is to die?
There are countless circumstances for death but fewer for life.
No one knows when, but all must meet death
like animals in a slaughterhouse.

É MA! After dying, consciousness doesn't cease
but gets caught, again and again, in the cycle of samsaric rebirth.
Wherever one is born, there is no time for true happiness.
In eighteen realms in hell, beings suffer from heat and cold,
hungry ghosts from thirst and hunger,
animals from eating each other.
Humans suffer over their mortality and
asura beings from constant war and killing.
Those in the heaven realm spend their lives indulgently
and die a terrible, lonely death.
Within the six realms, there is never true happiness or joy
but always the great suffering of being caught
in the midst of a flame.
Birth, like suffering, is a continuous and revolving cycle.
Therefore, one ought to have renunciation
for the suffering of samsara.

É MA! Happiness and suffering are created by karmic actions.
Karmic actions are like the painters of portraits.
Fruition of karmic actions is inevitable,
even after hundreds of eons.
What you have created, no others will experience.
What you have created cannot be changed.

Virtuous actions lead to travel in higher realms and liberation.
Unvirtuous actions lead to travel in lower realms and suffering.
Even if the cause is small, the fruition can ripen
with great intensity.
The realms and one's experience of them
are the result of one's own karmic deeds.

Therefore, at all times and in all situations,
the understanding of cause and effect is of the utmost importance.
One must be mindful of one's actions,
detailed and cautious, abandoning and creating
the right karmic conduct with determination.

É MA! Leaders of the liberation path are like magnificent lamps.
The teacher is the origin of all good qualities.
In these times of great degeneration,
the teacher is the true embodiment of the victorious buddhas.
Because the teacher is present at this time,
the teacher's kindness and blessings are even more beneficial.
Walking the path of Dharma without a teacher
is like a blind person walking a path
without a seeing person's help.
Therefore, the noble teacher is like a wish-fulfilling paksam tree.
And, to examine, choose, and then study with a teacher
is of great importance.
To nurture one's higher aspiration,
one must study the conduct of the noble beings
and meditate on the inseparably true nature of mind.
Fortunate beings who do this are never under
the influence of evils
and will be able to find the path;
the victorious buddhas will rejoice.

É MA! Peaceful liberation is a joyful state.
It is free from the chronic disease of samsara.
It is the end of samsara and its cause.

It is the destination of nonattachment and the noble path.
It is filled with the Victorious Ones and their sons and daughters,
the buddhas and bodhisattvas.
It is the resting place of arhats and pratyekabuddhas.
To practice the path of liberation diligently is the right thing.

É MA! The Three Jewels, incomparable and precious,
will never abandon you.
I myself take refuge in them and am content.
It is right to take refuge in them.
If you do this from the heart, they will never abandon you.
The Three Jewels can give one refuge
from the suffering of samsara.
The act of taking refuge itself is full of merit.
It can clear away the eight fears
and sixteen obstacles of this lifetime,
lead one from the lower realms,
and eventually from all suffering in the next.
Remember the Precious Jewels again and again,
and take refuge in them frequently.

É MA! This is the great path that has been traveled
by the Victorious Ones and their sons and daughters.
The incomparable bodhicitta mind
is the treasure of the noble beings.
Apply the two aspects of bodhicitta mind—
aspiring bodhicitta and engaged bodhicitta.
Only then will you receive the name
of son or daughter of the Victorious Ones.
Only then will you travel the joyful path to the joyful destination.
Ultimate and complete enlightenment is not far away.

Sentient beings of the three realms are one's kind parents.
They are unprotected and companionless
like a blind person in an open field.
Though they desire happiness,

they involve themselves in the sources of suffering.
You must wear great courage as your armor.
You must care for others more than for yourselves.
Take upon yourselves their sufferings,
and strive for their happiness.

One must practice diligently from the heart
the four limitless mind practices,
the six prajnas, and the four gathering mind practices.
It is said that all the conduct of the bodhisattvas,
the sons and daughters of the Victorious Ones,
is contained in these practices.
This purest of paths makes the bodhisattvas rejoice.
It is the purest essence of the essence heart.
So, please, hold it in your heart as precious.

É MA! For so long, we have dwelled in samsara.
From beginningless time, we have accumulated negative deeds.
Therefore, if one doesn't use the four powerful methods
to purify negative obscurations,
it is very difficult to free oneself
from the suffering of samsara.

Those who have arrived at the peaceful state of mind,
the buddhas and the lineage of root gurus,
are embodied in one form, the jeweled form.
Vajrasattva, who has the color of the moon or a white shell,
is seated on a moon disk, which rests upon a white lotus.
He is smiling. If one visualizes him
and recites the 100-syllable mantra,
all the negative forces and deeds will be eliminated,
and one will be liberated
and liberate others from the suffering of Narak [hell].

É MA! One who accumulates merit attains enlightenment.
One who does not will gain no excellent fruit.
Therefore, with intelligent methods, according to one's capacity,
one should use one's wealth to accumulate merit.
One should make mandala offerings
with visualizations to the three buddhafields.
One should offer a billion universes to the nirmanakaya,
countless buddhafields to the pure vision of the sambhogakaya,
and limitless pervasiveness to the dharmakaya.
In addition to this, one offers one's body,
wealth, and three-times' virtue to one's guru,
the embodiment of the Three Jewels,
and the kayas of the deity.
By doing so, one accumulates a great deal of merit
and exercises the clarity of one's vision.
It ripens one's ultimate wisdom, and the virtues are countless.
Therefore, the accumulation of merit is the main
source of practice.

É MA! From beginningless time, ignorance has caused
beings to grasp at an ego that ultimately doesn't exist.
Because of this, we dwell in the suffering of samsara.
Ultimately, there is no body, but we grasp at the body
as something inherently existent,
which results in aggression and attachment.
Therefore, this body of phenomena
to which we usually have a strong grip of attachment
is offered generously to the devils and demons
and all sentient beings.
By visualizing one's form as amrita, the demons are satisfied,
one accumulates merit, and one's karmic debts are paid.
This eliminates obstacles and disease.
One should dedicate the merit to all sentient beings.

Because all phenomena are dependent on one's motivation,
this visualization practice has merit
equal to offering one's own body.
It creates strong patterns of generosity
because it is virtuous and purifies obscurations.
One eventually recognizes one's own luminous
bardo wisdom.
One's life force is sustained, and disease
and demonic obstacles are eliminated.
Therefore, this is a wise offering that accumulates merit.
One should pray to the incomparable guru.

É MA! With great kindness, the guru has the natural quality
of the precious enlightened mind and holds the treasure
teachings of the three lineages with great blessing.
Visualizing him above one's head and inside one's heart
has merit equal to visualizing all of the buddhas.
One will receive the blessing of the three lineages in one's heart.
One will realize the inseparability of one's mind
and the guru's mind, and that is the ultimate nature.

There is nothing like guru yoga
to provoke one's ultimate state of mind.
One should receive the four initiations
from the three seed syllables (body, speech, and mind)
to eliminate the four obscurations.
This plants the seed that will make possible
the complete development of the four kaya states.
This empowers one to practice the four perfection paths
and to repair damaged samaya.
Ultimately, one sees the phenomena of samsara and nirvana
as the guru's state of mind and
exhausts unfavorable circumstances.
It fulfills one's wishes and makes firm the
kingdom of Dharmakaya
within this lifetime, or in the light of the Padma Field,
where one will travel the path of the four perfection stages.
Then one will become enlightened and immediately exhaust
one's kleshas, negativities, and ignorance.
One will benefit countless beings as vast as space,
and one will manifest kayas and
their luminosity, fully, without limit.

É MA! This is the path of the three transmission lineages
that the Victors of the Three Times have traveled upon,
the essential points of the 84,000 volumes
of the Buddha's teachings.
If 100 scholars and 1000 realized beings
came here spontaneously,
there still wouldn't be much more to teach than this.
This is the ambrosia of the Dharma.
These are the 1000 sangha practice points.
Teaching and listening to this path,
whatever merit there may be,
I pray that all sentient beings travel on this path,
and, in one lifetime, achieve enlightenment.

The sage benefited beings by his teachings, appearance, and kindness because of the ability of beings to hear, think about, see, and touch him. And, in a remote place called Mikmin, which means "ripened eye," he attained the full rainbow body.

Commentary on Part Two

Dabyang and Ngakyen go to Dhunkun Drubpa and ask him to teach them. In reality, Dhunkun Drubpa was Patrul Rinpoche's own teacher, Jigme Gyalwe Nyugu, who was himself renowned and whose teachings are still revered today. Patrul Rinpoche refers to him here as a sage. In Tibetan the word for *sage* is *drongson*. *Drong* means "straight," and *son* means "sustaining." Together they mean "someone who sustains the straightness and never lies."

The two bees prostrate and make offerings to him, as is traditional, and in the course of their conversation they see that he truly has the qualities of the Buddha, namely that his mind is not caught in ego-clinging and worldly confirmations. They understand that he is a "lamp of Dharma" who holds the teachings that can dispel the darkness of ignorance. They also realize that he embodies the virtues of the sangha, the followers of the Buddha, in that he acts in accordance with what he knows and teaches, and only seeks to benefit others. The Buddha, Dharma, and Sangha are referred to as the Three Jewels since they can overcome the impoverished suffering that results from wandering ceaselessly in a state of ignorance and can convey the true richness of liberation. For teachers to be completely authentic, they must possess the characteristics of all three.

Jigme Gyalwe Nyugu was very pleased. His teachings that follow are a summary of the entire Buddhist path. He begins by offering a prostration to the Buddha and to all the great bodhisattvas who have conquered the kleshas. The kleshas are ignorance, passion, and aggression—the three basic ways we stay rooted in our attachment to impermanent phenomena. At the same time, they're also the fundamental way that we look for happiness, and thus remain trapped in pain and the struggle to escape pain. In some ways, ignorance, passion, and aggression can be seen as the actual cause of any conceivable mode of existence. Since by practicing the Buddha's teachings one can free oneself from these entrapments, the Buddha is called the "Great Liberator of Beings." Jigme Gyalwe Nyugu supplicates the Buddha for "the minds of the six realms to turn toward the Dharma," so all sentient beings may be liberated.

He begins his teachings by outlining what are called in various traditions the four reminders, or the four mind changings, which are: the preciousness of having a fortunate human birth, the certainty of death, the ceaselessness of suffering, and the reality of karma—cause and effect. In the ordinary ways we humans go about our daily activities, we take for granted that we have plenty of time to do what we want. When we experience discomfort, restlessness, pain, or depression, we assume that if we work hard, we'll get what we want and achieve some stable state of happiness. We don't believe that our acts of self-indulgence, laziness, private hypocrisy, and unkindness will have any results in the grand scheme of things. That is, as we lead our ordinary lives, we ignore the reality of these four thoughts, and because we ignore them, we find ourselves prey to all kinds of anxieties, fears, and uncertainties. We do not feel that we're really in touch with our lives. These four thoughts are called *reminders* because they bring our attention back to the true facts of life that enable us to work with our situation in a genuine, meaningful, and profitable way. The four thoughts are also called *mind changings* because when we take them to heart, we can actually change our minds and free ourselves from the hopeful reliance on ignorant delusions. So Jigme Gyalwe Nyugu begins by talking about these four things.

The first is the preciousness of finding a well-favored human birth. We already talked about this a little. It's worth noting that if we think about all the sentient beings on this earth—insects, fish, birds, reptiles, warm-blooded animals—out of all those billions of creatures, a human birth is comparatively rare. It's by virtue of the humans' dominance over other creatures that such a birth is relatively fortunate. And if we don't have major physical or mental impairments that consume all our energy simply to live, that is certainly good fortune. Also, we are most fortunate if we are not born in a place where there is terrible famine, disease, ceaseless warfare, or oppressive tyranny, all of which deprive one's life of any freedom. Beyond that, it is the greatest good fortune if one lives in a time and place where one can receive teachings on the true nature of reality and on the practical methods of freeing oneself from delusion and suffering.

To receive such teachings from a living Buddha who exemplifies them and to follow the path in the company of others—in other words, if one encounters the Buddha, Dharma, and Sangha, the Three Jewels—then that is truly the meaning of having a "precious human birth, free and well-favored." In this context, Jigme Gyalwe Nyugu emphasizes the rare and decisive importance of encountering the Three Jewels.

In speaking of the certainty and suddenness of death, Jigme Gyalwe Nyugu says that "deluded, suffering, samsaric beings grasp at composite, impermanent things as if they were everlasting." Particularly in the West, aspects of physical reality are taken to be the "real" reality, including both the outer phenomena of buildings and trees, and also our own bodies. As everybody knows, these phenomena are made up of other things—elements, molecules, atoms, subatomic particles, and a vast amount of space. These elements appear in one form and then another, continuously, sometimes as part of ourselves and sometimes as other.

Nonetheless, for the purposes of perpetuating our own ignorance, we make all our plans by relying on the continuity of one form or another. Jigme Gyalwe Nyugu further makes the point that even the underlying elements—here, according to Eastern tradition, earth, water, fire, air, and space—are temporary, and the beings that rely on them will perish. Air pollution, lakes drying up, and volcanos destroying islands are obvious examples, but he is also saying that these elements are actually temporary concepts, dependent on a perceiver, and will therefore also dissipate. "Who knows where and when one is to die?" he asks, and concludes by insisting on the pervasive and sudden threat of death that none will escape.

Nor do our problems and our suffering end with death. Just as in life we go from one mental state to another, our consciousness changes but does not stop when we go from one place to another. Just as our consciousness came with us as we grew from babies into children, from teenagers into adults, middle-aged and then old, in each of these ages our bodies had quite different characteristics. We had at each of those times altogether different worries, interests, and thoughts. In this way, our consciousness will continue through death. Just because we cannot imagine a state of affairs without a personal consciousness and some kind of embodiment for that consciousness, nevertheless our consciousness will circulate from birth to birth.

As Jigme Gyalwe Nyugu then says, "Wherever one is born, there is no time for true happiness." To emphasize the complete suffering that inevitably accompanies the struggles of a reality based on birth and death, he refers to the eighteen realms of hell and the six realms—in other words, all the conceivable modes of existence. We began to talk about the realms, particularly the god and human realms, but it might be good at this point to go into more detail.

According to Buddhist tradition, there are three overall realms in phenomena: the desire, form, and formless realms. There are six desire realms, thirty-two form or heaven realms, and four formless realms. Those in the form realms have meditation, so their emotions are much happier and less confused. Above these, at the "top" of samsara, are four formless realms where beings live in meditative absorption of four different kinds. Buddhists believe that Hinduism and other religions are able to get that far but that they're not able to attain realization of egolessness. They are able to accumulate merit, but when that changes, they will fall back into the desire realm. These formless realms are a precise consciousness, such as awareness of the essence of samsara being like space. Beings can remain in such realms for eons. Above the formless realms is the essence of samsara, nothingness. Beings here cling to that consciousness and remain in it for eons. Above that, the most refined essence of samsara is that consciousness is not existent, and it is not nonexistent. This is pretty much like Buddhist philosophy, but it is not, because those with this belief remain in that absorption itself.

What about the desire realm? Within the six realms there is never true happiness or joy but always the great suffering of being caught "in the midst of a flame." Within the six realms are the god realm, the asura or jealous god realm, and the human realm. These three are the higher realms of samsara. In the lower realms are the animal realm, the hungry ghost realm, and the hell realm.

In the hell realm are eight hot hells and eight cold hells. The eight hot hells are stacked one on top of the other, with the Maximum Torture Hell at the bottom and the Reviving Hell at the top. This top hell realm is dark but because of karmic interdependence, the occupants can sense other beings. They are burning on a ground of red-hot iron and fight continually with other beings. Whenever the beings in this realm reach out, they get different weapons created by their karmic illusion and kill one another. But they immediately revive and begin their battle again.

The bodies of the beings in the Black Line Hell are placed on the base of a red-hot flat iron. The karmic rulers of these beings write lines on their bodies and cut them with steel saws. The severed portions immediately rejoin and are again cut into pieces. There is no one there, but based on karmic interdependence, their projections create rulers who do this to the beings.

The beings in the Rounding Up and Crushing Hell are smashed between iron mountains that crush their bodies.

When the boulders are lifted the beings revive, only to have the boulders pound together again to flatten their bodies.

The Howling Hell has a red-hot iron house with no door. There is fire inside, and beings cry out because they have to ceaselessly experience the physical and psychological pain of not being able to get out.

In the Loud Howling Hell, beings are driven into a chamber within a chamber, both made of flaming iron. The beings scream to get out but realize that even if they could escape from the inner chamber, there's no escape from the outer.

In the Heating Hell, beings are boiled in molten bronze, which is contained in a huge iron pot. Whenever the beings surface, they are seized by iron hooks, causing them to lose consciousness.

In the Intense Heating Hell, in a metal chamber filled with fire, the bodies of the beings are pierced with a burning iron trident, which enters both soles of the feet and the lower orifice, emerging through both shoulders and the crown of their head. They are wrapped in red-hot iron blankets and suffer tremendous torture.

The Maximum Torture Hell is an iron room of blazing fire, and beings are placed in the midst of iron blocks, which are heaped like red-hot coals as high as a mountain. The bodies and the flames burn as one with no chance of escape. When the flames subside, beings attempt to run away, but they are struck by large arrows, sticks, and hammers, and molten bronze is poured into their mouths.

All beings die and live in the mind. So, after they die, they hear the sound of life. These are regular experiences of mind and are very claustrophobic.

The eight cold hells all have similar physical features, basically lands composed of snow-covered mountains and ice-filled valleys, where blizzards constantly and furiously rage. These cold hells are marked by loneliness.

In the Blistered Hell, the naked beings grow physically weaker as blisters rapidly appear on their bodies. The Blister-Bursting Hell is so cold that the blisters burst and ulcerate. The unbearable biting cold in the Teeth-Chattering Hell makes the beings' teeth chatter. The Oh! Cold! Hell is so-called because beings are so afflicted by the cold that they scream ceaselessly. In the Uttering of "Alas" Hell, after losing the strength of their voices, the victims can only sigh, "Alas! Alas!" In the Cracking Like a Blue Poppy Hell, the outer skin of the beings turns blue and cracks into four parts, like the petals of a blue poppy. In the Cracking Like a Lotus Hell, beings are frozen by the cold, and the inner red flesh beneath their skin is exposed and cracks into eight parts, like the petals of a red lotus. In the Cracking Like a Large Lotus Hell, here the skin of beings turns red and black, cracking into sixteen, then thirty-two, and then innumerable parts. Maggots with iron mandibles enter their wounds caused by the cracks and feed there. Thus, beings suffer intensely from the tortures of the cold.

There are also four sets of neighboring hells that surround the Maximum Torture Hell at each of the four cardinal directions. As beings emerge from the Maximum Torture Hell, those in the Burning Bed of Live Coals observe a far-off, dense shadow of darkness and happily go toward it, but they fall into a hot bed of ashes with fire burning furiously beneath it, which burns their flesh and bones. The beings in the Marsh of Putrefied Corpses have been roasting in fire for eons since the disintegration and destruction of the previous great cycle, so they're very thirsty. They are happy to see water, but when they approach it to drink, instead they sink head deep into a marsh composed entirely of dead bodies—human corpses, the carcasses of horses, dogs, and the like, which are rotting, putrid, and crawling with maggots. There they are eaten by the different creatures who eat flesh and chew bones, and have the constant sensation of falling down and then getting up, then down, then up.

After escaping from the marsh, beings in the Meadow of Weapons see a delightful green meadow. Approaching it, they come upon a field of weapons and find the entire meadow overgrown with red-hot, grass-like, iron blades. Setting down their right foot, their right foot is pierced; setting down their left foot, their left foot is pierced. Their feet heal when lifted, but upon setting them down again, they are cut as before.

Again, after escaping from the meadow, they see a Forest of Swords, which appears delightful, so they run toward it. But instead of finding an inviting forest, it's made of iron trees with leaves that grow like swords. As the wind moves them, the swords cut the beings' bodies into pieces. The pieces rejoin as before, and thus they suffer the pain of being repeatedly cut. On the Hill of Iron Trees with Sharp, Pointed Leaves, adulterers and reprobate monks and nuns, who have been unfaithful to one another or have broken their vows, are born. As the force of their karma draws them before the dreadful Hill of Iron Trees, they hear their former lovers calling to them from the top of the hill. As they ascend, all the leaves of the iron trees point downward and pierce them. When they reach the top of the hill, hawks and vultures pluck out their eyes. Again, they hear enticing voices, but this time from the foot of the hill. When the descending victims approach as before, all the leaves of the trees point upward and pierce straight through the center of their chests and out their backs. As they move toward the foot of the hill, dreadful iron male and female figures embrace them and chew their heads in their mouths. The beings suffer the torture of seeing their own white brain tissue oozing from the corners of these monsters' jaws. All of this is a play of your mind.

In the hungry ghost realm are two different kinds of hungry ghosts, the flying hungry ghosts and the hungry ghosts with hallucination. Their legs are like small straws, their neck like a pin. Because they have had no food for years and years, their legs and feet cannot support their bellies, and their necks cannot support their heads, but they try. Because of their lack of food, they have hallucinations and are burning inside from hunger. They see water and go toward it, but it's nothing but fire. They see food, but it's nothing but fire and weapons that cut their bodies. Then there's a beautiful place almost like a heaven realm, but as soon as they try to get there, it also turns into fire and weapons that cut their bodies.

The flying hungry ghosts are angry local spirits filled with negativity. Unless they have met Padmasambhava, most of them are violent, and after their time in this realm, they go to the hell realm. Just as hell is marked by anger and passion, the hungry ghost realm is marked by stinginess, poverty mentality, and resentment.

In the animal realm are sea and earth animals, domestic and wild. Animals suffer in that they do not have one second of peace because they're afraid, and their lives are constantly threatened. They are also used in the fields and must carry heavy loads.

These are all mind conditions. The fruition of these mind conditions is feeling them to be absolutely solid, and this is confirmed by one's previous karmic deeds. In each of these realms, one feels that they are real.

Then there is the human realm where the baby in the mother's womb suffers, and during birth, both the mother and baby unavoidably suffer. As soon as you're born, you are aging, your body deteriorates with some sickness, and then ultimately you die. These are the unavoidable sufferings of the human realm—birth, old age, sickness, and death, along with mental emotions, aggression, and passion.

In the asura realm there is one wish-fulfilling tree with its roots in the ocean. In the middle of the tree is the asura realm; the top of the tree is in the heaven realm. Because all the fruit of the tree is in heaven, the asuras in the middle are jealous that only those in the heaven realm can enjoy the fruit of the wish-fulfilling tree. Emotionally, they always want to attack and kill those in the heaven realm. Yet when they attack, mostly they lose and are killed. Even when they're not fighting, they're unable to rest their minds because of their jealousy. It is believed that in the heaven realm, beings have amrita, an anti-death medicine. If somebody dies, amrita could restore their life. But the asura realm doesn't have amrita, so the heaven realm always wins, which causes the asuras to constantly suffer.

In the heaven realm, suffering occurs because the gods have beautiful possessions, such as palaces, and they're always indulging in pleasurable things, yet they have no sense of impermanence at all. Even though from the four sides of the heaven realm's palace teachings arise in the sound of a constantly beating drum, because nobody wants to hear the teachings, no one pays attention. However, before they die the gods begin to have experiences they hadn't had before. They start to sense smells they hadn't smelled before. Flowers become old and begin to rot, whereas before new flowers would appear. The other gods start to keep their distance when this happens, and the dying god becomes isolated. When the gods realize they are about to die, they experience tremendous pain from having to leave the pleasurable heaven realm. Most who die in the heaven realm go to the hell realm. With their sudden realization of impermanence and seeing where they're going, they experience tremendous pain, because by then they've exhausted all their karmic merit and now have mostly negative karma to resolve, which is why they go to the hell realm. The eyes of gods in the heaven realm have tremendous clarity, so they're able to see far into the future, which is even more painful to them because they have no choice but to follow their karmic situation.

Happiness and suffering are created by karmic actions. *Karma* means "actions." It was one of the Buddha's great insights that all actions have results, and the chain reaction of action and result is ceaseless. According to Buddhist belief, all of samsara is created by karmic deeds or actions. The different realms are the fruition of karmic deeds in relation to mind and the objects of mind.

Though the nature of the mind has no beginning nor causes or conditions, the structure of the mind is dependent on karmic deeds. Human mind is dependent on human deeds, and the structure of the mind in the different realms is conditioned by deeds appropriate to that realm. External things, such as the realms themselves, are also created by collective karmic deeds, so there's no such thing inherently outside of karmic deeds. One way to demonstrate this is the example of a human looking at water and seeing it as a drink, whereas a fish sees water as a place to live. This shows that water does not exist inherently as one thing, or both beings would relate to it the same way. Water has its own quality, and that quality is not inherently existent. It comes from the void, and how it comes from the void is different for different beings. You cannot separate the qualities from the experience.

Karma is the entire structure of your mind, and everything is a production of karma. All the beings of the six realms share the same nature of mind, but their structure of mind is different because of differing specific karma. Things that the various occupants experience are different because of different karmic deeds. Everything is the result of prior actions, and karma is the substance of everything, so we cannot envision other realms' phenomena because those actions and perceptions are not our own. If we try to relate to other realms with our own perceptions, it's difficult. But we can understand through the Buddha's teachings because the Buddha has seen the six realms simultaneously—how they are manufactured by different karma. So, through these teachings we can relate to the suffering and experiences of beings in other realms.

This is a very important teaching in the Madhyamika: Every appearance is mind. In the Nyingma tradition, there are two schools; one says "Everything is mind," and the other says "Appearance is mind." If everything is mind, then when you die everything has to die, and obviously that's not the case. If one falls asleep, then everything should vanish, and that's not the case. Appearance is one's mind. For example, the picture of this cup is mind. I see a picture of this cup, and that is my mind, but the cup itself is not my mind. It is a product of my mind because of my previous deeds. How it arises from the void is according to one's deeds.

Gampopa summarized the suffering of the higher realms as follows. The misery of happy existence is threefold: that of human beings, asuras, and gods. Humans suffer birth, sickness, old age, and death. The asuras remain unsatisfied by sensual enjoyment, are humiliated, killed, violated, slaughtered, and banished. They suffer death and transformation and fall into lower forms of life. When a god dies, there are five omens. Their clothing becomes soiled; their garland of flowers fades; perspiration breaks forth from their armpits; an evil smell arises from their body, and their seat, which was always comfortable, becomes uncomfortable. This type of misery of transmigration does not exist in the form and formless realms. Here, when their merit is exhausted and they awaken from their samadhi, they are instantly reborn in a lower realm, where the misery of that existence is then experienced.

Therefore, at all times and in all situations, the understanding of cause and effect is of utmost importance. Wherever you're born, there is no place where you can be comfortable and relax. Everything is like being born in a place surrounded by fire, so that wherever you go, you can't escape that ring of fire, and the suffering continuously attracts you. Seeing this situation very clearly, it makes sense that you must completely renounce the suffering of samsara.

All of these experiences and ways of being are the result of karma, which is the fourth mind-changing thought that Jigme Gyalwe Nyugu takes up. Everything one experiences, including one's experience of one's own mind, is the fruition of previous karma. Everything that you experience, no matter what realm you're in, is the fruition of previous deeds. But how you *react* is the seed of future karma. The human realm provides more choices for sustaining strength and not reacting. In the hell realm, beings kill each other, but that doesn't have the same result as it does for humans because the condition of their mind is formed in that way, so there is a subtle result. How one reacts is the cause of future karma.

Again, karma is nothing outside but is within one's mental continuum, which has continued from beginningless time and is continuing still. Karma has three rules. First, it will never miss its own fruition, meaning that even if a long period of time passes, once the causes and conditions for that seed to ripen are present, that seed will ripen and fruit without fail. Second, it will not ripen its fruition to another mental continuum, which means that the mental continuum that has created the karma will not ripen on someone else's mental continuum. And third, one cannot take on other people's karma. If this were possible the buddhas and bodhisattvas would have done this many times over already.

How karma actually happens is that within one's own mental continuum, the good karma is less ignorant, feels more positive, and is the result of good intention. There is less ignorance in the sense that if I have a strong compassionate feeling, this compassionate feeling is less ignorant because I understand the suffering nature. I am not ignorant of my own suffering nature and thus have an awareness of relative samsara. Part of the feeling of compassion is feeling a strong responsibility for other people's suffering, so it's a pleasurable feeling even though it's sad to see other people suffering. To have the vision to seize other people's mental suffering is naturally very joyful. And then when you help somebody to get out of suffering, such as giving them money or food, such acts always present a good fruition. The nature of that mind as awareness, the feeling as joy, and the act that arises from it will always present you with good fruition. Therefore, compassion and generosity are always positive. Whatever happens in your mental continuum will carry forward in your mind. Your mental continuum will experience that act; you won't miss it.

In contrast, the nature of anger is ignorance. Insensitivity is ignorance and anger, so its nature is suffering. When you get angry, it's not pleasurable. Compassion is pleasurable because it is not limited by egoistic fears and ambitions. Acting out of anger or killing derives from the experience of suffering in the past mental continuum; therefore, such an act is negative. You can also see that in this lifetime. If you have been generous, people act nicely to you; therefore, your mental continuum immediately experiences the result of the act. If you are mean, people are not nice to you. Therefore, you experience it on the spot. But you can also experience it later in the lower realms. For those reasons, we experience the result of what is negative or positive. Any self-defense gives rise to negative emotions such as anger, jealousy, attachment, ignorance, and arrogance, all of which come from self-protection.

Kindness and compassion come from helping others. So basically, caring for others is the seed for all positive qualities that can arise in one's mind, and self-clinging is the seed of all the negative qualities because it is ignorance and displeasure, and it will have bad results. It is ignorant because there is no such self.

We have a view of self as permanent, independent, and singular, and there is no such object that is permanent, independent, and singular. Thus, it is just ignorant clinging to something that does not really exist. Its object does not exist, and therefore such clinging causes displeasure because it is dependent on hope and fear. It is pain or illusion. For example, when you say, "I am here," there is nothing really "there" to be touched. How we "touch" anything with our sensory experience is all based on habitual clinging. So, the nature of self-clinging is ignorance because there is no self.

Feeling itself is defiled, or *takpa*, because it is rooted in dualism and therefore gives rise to either hope or fear, and the result is bad because anger arises from it. Caring for others has the opposite effect. You don't care about a table or a stone. When you care for someone, you're caring for their emotions, the mental continuum, which exists relatively. So, awareness and caring are not unpleasant. The nature of caring is awareness because the mind is aware of the other's relative existence, and it is pleasant because you let go of your egotistical mind. Your mind is in a more natural state, and the result is always good because you can express it with love and kindness and compassion.

That's how karma works, and the body and speech more or less help the mind, but the one that really acts is the mind.

It is the mental continuum that experiences its own previous deeds. There are two karmas: immediate and lifetimes later. It can happen either way, but there is *always* a result. Karma is not dependent on anything else. It arranges itself all the time. Karma is the activity of the mind, and it is endless. If one understands that this is the case, then it stands to reason that one would seek out a teacher who has faced these things squarely and found the true means of liberation. In this age, that teacher is the Gautama Buddha. One who has ascertained the truth of his teachings should take refuge in him, his teachings, and his followers, and renounce finding refuge in any conventional worldly aims, means, or guidance.

Once again, Jigme Gyalwe Nyugu refers to the teacher as a lamp in a dark room. "É MA! Leaders of the liberation path are like magnificent lamps." When there is a lamp in a dark room, one can clearly see others and objects. Similarly, in samsara, when there are those involved with ignorant karmic kleshas, the teacher introduces prajna, and the teacher's words clarify the ignorant mind and purify that ignorance, bringing a luminous and clear understanding of one's path. Therefore, the teacher is a lamp, and one comes to depend on the teacher's words. Then you can see what to accept and what to reject, what is the cause of suffering, and what is the cause of joy and happiness. Furthermore, you see how to eliminate suffering and to cultivate freedom. The teacher's words are the lamp that shows you the direction. The teacher is the origin of all good qualities. In these times of great degeneration, the teacher is the true embodiment of the victorious buddhas.

From the teachings, one can cultivate prajna, and with prajna abandon all negative qualities and bad habitual patterns, and instead cultivate profound, brilliant, and glorious qualities. Since the teacher is the origin of all good qualities, "the noble teacher is like a wish-fulfilling paksam tree." Therefore, to examine, choose, and then study with a teacher is of great importance. If the teacher is highly accomplished, that means that the teacher's dharmakaya realization is totally inseparable from the dharmakaya mind of all enlightened beings. There is no such thing as two dharmakayas. Because there are not two enlightened natures, such a teacher has the communicative sambhogakaya qualities. And because the teacher's nirmanakaya qualities are equally enriched, the teacher is an enlightened being, even though that teacher may seem to be ordinary.

Sentient beings experience the Buddha according to their karmic obscurations. Those sentient beings who have fewer karmic obscurations will be able to see more of the excellent qualities of enlightened mind. Those who have more obscurations experience fewer of these excellent qualities. Our experience is totally dependent on our karmic conditions. So, when we see a teacher who seems ordinary, it's not because the teacher is ordinary; it's because of our karmic obscuration. If that teacher leads us to the enlightened path, they actually have such profound compassion that they could relate to us even more than the other buddhas of the past, present, or future. The teacher can relate to us personally, individually, even though we have such karmic kleshas. So, this teacher has extreme compassion in appearing and in making themselves able to relate with us. This teacher might have taken us in their heart very deeply, not only in this lifetime but for many generations. And the teacher didn't let go of us but always sought us. Such teachers exist in the degenerate times, and they show us the enlightened path.

The paksam tree symbolizes the teacher as the origin of all good things. This tree exists in the heavenly realm and spontaneously gives to disciples whatever they pray for or need. To the disciples and students who don't lack devotion and trust, blessings will arise from the teachers and fulfill their desire to eliminate suffering and cultivate the enlightened mind.

Nevertheless, it is important to examine the teacher. The first thing to find out is whether the teacher has the transmission of a profound, unbroken lineage. And if so, one should find out whether the teacher is practicing or has accomplished what they are teaching. One may not be able to see the teacher's mind, but their conduct will be evident, so examine that. The second thing to do when you find a real teacher who has noble qualities from practicing the profound lineage is to practice with the teacher in the three pleasing ways. These three pleasing ways begin by receiving the complete initiation and the blessings. The first pleasing way is the lowest: you offer wealth and material things. The second or intermediate level is to offer your body, speech, and mind. The third or highest is the most important thing—to offer your whole life toward practice, which is the ultimate thing you can do.

The idea of offering material things and body, speech, and mind completely to the teacher is not so that the teacher can take you on as a slave and make use of you for their own purposes. But it is true that if a student is completely devoted and offers their material things, as well as body, speech, and mind, then the student at first does become somewhat fragile. But then their egotistical, negative habitual patterns dissolve, and they're able to observe the prajna of the teachings and receive the true blessings of the teacher.

Finally, do not waste a minute of your time in this precious human body, and completely dedicate yourself to doing the practice, becoming enlightened, and benefiting all beings. Until you have the wisdom to judge, even if you see some negative things in the teacher, that should not distract you from your devotion, but rather it should be a source of cultivating your own pure perception. So, the first thing one must do is to examine the teacher very clearly before taking them as your teacher. Second, take the teachings, and study and practice with the teacher to learn everything about the practice to make sure that you have everything that they got from the practice. Then make sure that your mind and the teacher's mind are inseparable, and rest in the inseparability of your mind and the teacher's mind, in the meeting of naturalness. If you take this advice, you will never experience obstacles or be destroyed by any demon. You will achieve the path that all the buddhas and bodhisattvas rejoice in.

"É MA! Peaceful liberation is a joyful state. It is free from the chronic disease of samsara." Jigme Gyalwe Nyugu describes this path as being free from samsara and its opposite, nirvana. It leads to the peaceful liberation that is the dwelling place of the buddhas and bodhisattvas who work ceaselessly for the liberation of all beings, and is the resting place of the arhats and pratekyabuddhas. *Arhat* refers to "one who has conquered the enemies." In Tibetan, the word for arhat is *dachom, da* meaning "enemy" and *chom* meaning "seized or destroyed." Thus, an arhat is "one who has destroyed the source of dwelling in the suffering of samsara."

Beings dwell in the suffering of samsara because of ego-clinging. The arhats understand egolessness and have conquered the gross negative emotions; they have overcome negative karmic interdependence. According to the Hinayana view, when they die, they will face the disappearance of atoms into the sky and consciousness into space, and then they will be liberated. According to the Mahayana, the arhats will not be completely liberated because they still have some ego-clinging. Because of that ignorance, they will again accumulate subtle karma, but they will follow the subtle accumulations and become completely enlightened. The pratyekabuddhas actually practice with a real teacher for two lifetimes. For example, they'll see a bone, and from seeing that bone will think about interdependent origination and come to understand that it all comes from ignorance. They will realize this wisdom and become enlightened. The arhats understand the emptiness of the gross things of phenomena, the atoms and consciousness, but the pratyekabuddhas understand the emptiness of atoms and consciousness completely, so their view is a little higher, though they still cling to their understanding.

"É MA! The Three Jewels, incomparable and precious, will never abandon you . . . It is right to take refuge in them." As Jigme Gyalwe Nyugu says, one enters this path by taking refuge. The way of proceeding on the path is nonattachment and renunciation, and the result is peace and freedom from the sufferings of samsara. This is a summary of the refuge section, and it is the essence of the Hinayana path.

Following this, Jigme Gyalwe Nyugu outlines the more expansive path of the bodhisattva or Mahayana vehicle. "E MA! This is the great path that has been travelled by the Victorious Ones and their sons and daughters. The incomparable bodhicitta mind is the treasure of the noble beings." In the Hinayana, one aspires to attain the level of an arhat. In the Mahayana, one aspires to be a bodhisattva, capable not only of liberating oneself but of liberating all sentient beings from the condition of suffering.

The key to treading on the Mahayana path is the development of bodhicitta. *Bodhi* means "awakened" or "enlightened," and *citta* means "mind" or "heart," so the process of developing bodhicitta is to awaken what is already in your heart. We begin with the two aspects of what is called "relative bodhicitta" to realize the absolute or completely unconditional awakened state. Anything that is a concept or substance is relative because it only can be said to exist in relation to other concepts or substances.

The two aspects of relative bodhicitta are generating or aspiration bodhicitta and engaged bodhicitta. Aspiration bodhicitta is the wish to attain enlightenment in order to free sentient beings from the suffering of samsara. In other words, to benefit sentient beings, one wishes for their enlightenment. This wish is for others and not for oneself. The aim here is to regard all sentient beings as having been your mother, dedicated to your care. They have sought the best for you and devoted themselves to protecting you from all harmful things. Realizing that is important, because only on that basis can we cultivate some kind of genuine care for all beings, which can engender the wish for all beings to be happy, not just for a day or two, but forever. This will only happen if they become enlightened by eliminating the cause of suffering and cultivating the awareness of their enlightened mind; this is our ultimate wish for them.

Practically speaking, what you can actually do for them is to guide them to the enlightened path. If you want to be able to do that, you first need to be enlightened yourself, so you have the wisdom to see all of the different beings' mental faculties and obscurations, and free them from that. So, from the beginning when you are motivated to become enlightened, you are not just trying to ease your own suffering; you're trying to accomplish something that could really help others to achieve ultimate happiness. When you have so much care for others, it's natural that you'd become free from suffering; you're just naturally taken care of.

As for engaged bodhicitta, it's not only that you have such a wish, but also that you engage in the practice, which makes you able to achieve enlightenment. It could be through the six paramitas. The first five are relative—generosity, discipline, patience, exertion, meditation—but the last one, prajna or wisdom, is absolute. Absolute bodhicitta is being completely free from dualistic conceptualizations and is sustained through awareness of emptiness. That is most important because understanding the absolute makes everything workable for the enlightened path, like the eyes of the body.

Until one has absolute bodhicitta, the sixth paramita, prajna, isn't true prajna but false, or conditional. When one has complete understanding of the absolute nature, then one starts to have complete prajna. The difference between complete prajna and false prajna is that false prajna can only be prajna with reference to interdependent origination. False prajna concerns dualistic actions, and complete prajna is the basis for action without dualistic, conceptual mind. You have a conceptual understanding of prajnaparamita but not a complete understanding of it. Until you have a realization of complete emptiness nature, you don't see how from emptiness everything appears and works interdependently as illusion. So, you still have a very strong sense of dualistic perception and grasping. Only if there is meritorious action taking place will there be any happiness in worldly activities that are, after all, interdependent and impermanent.

Another aspect of paramita practice is having complete confidence in the nondual state of mind. This brings further merit—inexhaustible merit—because emptiness nature is realized. The merit becomes inexhaustible and the basis for inexhaustible fruition, the rupakaya quality of buddhahood. Because substance and concepts are relative to each other, their reality is relative. That which is not substance and is beyond conception is absolute. The absolute nature is not graspable. As soon as you conceptualize, you are grasping. So, it is beyond subject and object, perceiver and perception.

One cannot describe the absolute nature through words and signs or by any act. But a description, though not strictly true, communicates something. It is complete freedom from conceptual fixation. This brings with it a great sense of bliss and also unceasing, unfixated luminosity, vast and pervasive. Again, this is not like a dead, cold vacuum. It is unceasing luminosity, which means that it is not object nor subject, but it is unceasing awareness. Because it is not object or subject, it has no nature of inherent suffering or pleasure but rather an extraordinary sense of bliss.

Bodhicitta mind in Tibetan is *changchub sem. Chang* means "dispersed" and *chub* means "compact." The negative is completely dispersed from the enlightened mind, which is compact with the positive. What is dispersed is ignorance and dualistic, habitual clinging. What is compactly pulled together is the sense of awareness and all the excellent, profound, brilliant qualities. The Tibetan word *semkyé* is defined as *sem*, or "mind," and *kyé*, which means "to arise." Nothing but mind arises spontaneously, so a mind that has arisen disperses its ignorant clinging while it draws together enlightened awareness.

In Tibetan, *mön* means "wish"; *sem*, "mind"; and *kyé*, "generating or arising," which is the "wish to get enlightened." *Mönpé semkyé* means "generating bodhicitta" or "aspiration bodhicitta." The Tibetan term *jukpa semkyé* means "engaged bodhicitta." The first is the wish to become enlightened for the benefit of all sentient beings, and the second is to engage in the enlightened practices of the six paramitas and so forth. When you are engaged, you might not be simultaneously thinking to become enlightened because you're involved in doing something. But that mind led you to engage, and the effect of the mind remains in your mental continuum, so it's still like arousing bodhicitta. For example, when you generously give something to somebody, and you don't think you're going to receive something in return, that mind led you to the act. The mind is affected by the act, which is included in the mind.

The six paramitas, again, are generosity, discipline, patience, exertion, meditation, and the absolute one is prajna. There are many places where you can read about these, so we don't need too much detail here. One must practice diligently, from the heart, the four limitless mind practices, the six paramitas, and the four magnetisms. Without the other practices, the six paramitas may not be entirely complete. You may not be able to really help others to get on an enlightened path. You may be patient or generous, and so forth, but are still not getting beings onto the path.

The four magnetisms are how you can cultivate the resources to bring beings onto the path of their own enlightenment. First, through generosity people will look to you as an example of a practitioner. Second, you would speak only with very gentle words and beautiful sentences, so students could relate to you without any awkwardness. Third, you'd teach them according to their mental abilities. You'd examine their mind, and teach them according to their ability. In this way, you'd bring them from their place to the enlightened path. Fourth, you'd practice in order to really have confidence in what you're teaching.

As to the four limitless or immeasurable mind practices, according to Buddhist belief, your parents and relatives *now* once were not your parents and relatives, and those who are not your parents or relatives now have been your relatives in previous lifetimes. Though in one lifetime your parents don't change, those who are close to you may become far away, and those who are far away may become very close to you.

In the future, these parents and relatives will not be so, and those who are not will one day be your relatives and parents. To hold any egotistical attachment for your closeness is illusory because the subject doesn't stay permanent. When you abandon this closeness and attachment to your ego, you have complete closeness to all the sentient beings who have been your mothers. According to Buddhist belief, this mental continuum has no beginning and throughout history rides on different forms of body; most of the body-forms have a mother, especially in this world.

We have taken countless lives in the human realm. Knowing that, you have equal care and concern for all sentient beings with no exceptions. This is the first limitless or immeasurable practice. Through your equanimity, your care for all sentient beings is limitless. The object is limitless; therefore, the care is limitless and has merit. The second practice is considering that all mother sentient beings want to be happy. Due to their ignorance about the cause of happiness, even though they don't want to suffer, they are very involved in causing their own suffering. So, when you genuinely care for them and wish them all to be happy, that is called *kindness*. Your kindness mind wishes all sentient beings to be happy. That motivation is based on limitless sentient beings; that kindness is limitless, so the merit is limitless. The third limitless practice is that all sentient beings don't want to suffer, but they are heavily involved in the cause of suffering. Realizing that, you have a genuine wish for them to be free from their suffering and the cause of suffering, and that is called *compassion*. That compassion motivation is based on limitless sentient beings; therefore, compassion is limitless and the merit is limitless. The fourth practice is limitless *rejoicing* in sentient beings' happiness, relative and ultimate. The rejoicing is limitless because sentient beings are limitless, and the merit is therefore limitless.

This can sound complicated, so for simplicity's sake, just talking about the relative level, we might say that the first category of bodhicitta, generating or aspiration bodhicitta, is developing the motivation to attain enlightenment to benefit sentient beings, and the second category, engaged bodhicitta, involves the practice of the six paramitas. Developing bodhicitta, you are a bodhisattva, and you travel the path of great joy until you achieve enlightenment.

Sentient beings of the three realms are one's kind parents. Somehow, all sentient beings are, have been, or will be your mother. Due to ignorance, these motherly sentient beings suffer in samsara. They desire comfort and joy, but not knowing what they are doing, they commit negative actions that produce suffering and emotional discomfort. They don't want emotional discomfort and suffering, but they don't know how to produce happiness with positive actions. So, what they do and what they want are in opposition. Thinking about their suffering, develop great compassion and kindness. Take the suffering of all sentient beings upon yourself, and give all your joy of any kind to them. With this courage and this great mind, you accumulate great merit. If you practice the six paramitas from your heart in this way, you will soon become enlightened. That finishes the practice of refuge and bodhicitta. Please take these teachings to heart.

Now for the practice of Vajrasattva. "É MA! For so long, we have dwelled in samsara. From beginningless time, we have accumulated negative deeds." Because of our past negative actions, we must experience the fruit of these negativities in the future. That is why we must purify our negativities through the practice of the Bodhisattva Vajrasattva. If we don't practice the path of the Bodhisattva Vajrasattva with its fourfold methods, we'll never have the chance to become enlightened or to escape the suffering of samsara. Those who have arrived at the peaceful state of mind—the buddhas and the lineage of root gurus—are embodied in one jeweled form, Vajrasattva, who is the color of the moon or a white shell.

How do we practice the Bodhisattva Vajrasattva? Vajrasattva is the embodiment of all the buddhas, and his nature is inseparable from our teacher's. His nature is the same as that of all the buddhas and bodhisattvas, the same as your lama's nature, but his appearance is that of Vajrasattva. His body is white, like a white shark, and he sits on top of a thousand-petalled lotus, on top of a moon. He is smiling. He has two hands. In his right hand he holds a vajra, and in his left, he holds a bell at his hip. He is embracing his consort, who sits on his lap. Of the fourfold methods, or the four powers, this visualization is the first.

The second method is remembering all of your negative actions and regretting those actions. The third method is making the promise not to create any more negativities, and you will be free from samsara. The fourth method is reciting the mantra of Vajrasattva. Because of the great importance and value of these four powerful methods, I'd like to go into them in a little more detail.

Negative karmic obscurations are the fruition of previous deeds, and they can only be purified by the four powerful methods, which are as follows. First, visualize Vajrasattva above your head. He's powerful, so by visualizing him, you're motivated to become enlightened to purify all sentient beings' negative deeds. The second is confessing your previous negative deeds by completely realizing how negative they are. This is powerful because negative deeds are created by ignorance, so you are accepting that you're ignorant, yet you have the wisdom to see how the deeds are negative. The third power is the power of resolve, which is promising not to create any more negative kleshas because you completely realize their effect on you, so you don't want to take any other chances. That is powerful because it's genuine confession. By the time you've confessed, you have realized its effect, like tasting the poison and seeing how bad it is, and knowing you won't take it again. You face how bad it is. First, you confess how bad it was, even though you wanted very much for it to happen. That's honesty. And then you have, more or less, complete awareness and confidence, so you don't do that anymore.

Reciting the mantra is the fourth method. While visualizing the mantra in Vajrasattva's heart and receiving nectar from the place of union with his consort, nectar streams down through the lotus stem into your consciousness, purifying it. Reciting the mantra is powerful because the mantra is the name of Vajrasattva, which itself carries many blessings. The mantra is a profound and provoking means for receiving blessings from the deity. It is important to understand that Vajrasattva is not some sort of outside entity or conventional god who, when you call on him and do the right kinds of things to please him, will come from some other realm to help you. The point is that Vajrasattva, which means "indestructible being" or "diamond-like being," is the self-existing principle of complete purity. This purity has never been stained or colored by anything; also, it has never been subject to increase or diminution. It is always there. Vajrasattva's presence, despite our own mental obscurations, is absolute and constant. That purity contains the power of compassionate action, which is never subject to any kind of ego-clinging or any petty-minded, fearful considerations, or reliance on any form of duality whatsoever. So, it is within us all, and we do the practice of Vajrasattva to uncover and actualize the indestructible purity of the bodhisattva's way.

Next, there is the mandala offering. To proceed on the bodhisattva's path and to fully actualize the ability to liberate each and every sentient being, one must acquire merit. Merit has the ability to completely cut through ego-clinging, grasping, and fixation of any kind. "É MA! One who accumulates merit attains enlightenment. One who does not will gain no excellent fruit." If you don't accumulate merit, there is no way to achieve enlightenment. That is why you must use a skillful method in order to accumulate merit. Accumulating merit here is making offerings of anything you can visualize— including the nirmanakaya buddhafield, the sambhogakaya buddhafield, the dharmakaya buddhafield, your own body, wealth, and whatever you have—to the Three Precious Jewels, your guru, dakinis, deities, and protectors. This is the mandala offering. If you accumulate merit, it will make you have even more merit to create your own buddhafield. It will purify your negativities and create so much more merit, which is why accumulating merit is very important.

With visualizations, one should make offerings of mandalas to the three buddhafields. In the enlightened path one must accumulate two different kinds of merit, relative merit and absolute merit. Relative merit provides proper opportunities to realize the absolute nature and for that to purify negative obscurations. Absolute merit sustains the awareness of emptiness nature in deep meditation. These two ways of accumulating merit are the only ways to attain profound, brilliant, and glorious buddhahood, which is the three kayas.

Mandala practice makes an offering of three-kaya objects to one's own guru, to the lineage refuge objects, and to the three-kaya objects. One should offer a billion universes to the nirmanakaya, countless buddhafields to the pure vision of the sambhogakaya, and limitless pervasiveness to the dharmakaya. The "three thousand universes" means the desire, form, and formless realms. It doesn't literally mean "three thousand" but refers to the desire, form, and formless realms as one universe, and one thousand of those are a thousand universes. That many universes equal one nirmanakaya buddhafield, which can benefit that many beings. We make an offering of "three thousandfold" universes to our own root guru and refuge objects, along with our body, speech, mind, and wealth as well, in order to achieve nirmanakaya qualities.

Our ordinary perception cannot see the sambhogakaya realm; only a buddha can experience it. In the nirmanakaya, buddhas appear and disappear. But in the sambhogakaya, buddhas always appear; they never disappear. In the nirmanakaya realm, the teachings appear and disappear, and there are many different kinds of teachings, direct and indirect. In the sambhogakaya, the teachings don't disappear, and they're always true Mahayana teachings. In the nirmanakaya realm, the disciples have impure perception and thus still have something to perfect, so it's ordinary. But in the sambhogakaya, the disciples are equally as realized as the teacher, the main buddha, because only buddhas are there. In the nirmanakaya realm, time is divided into past, present, and future, and in the sambhogakaya, there is no time of past, present, and future. It is ongoing, beyond conceptual divisions of time and place, with all the excellent qualities and symbols of Buddha's wisdom.

Where does this sambhogakaya buddhafield exist, and what is the role of the students if all are equally realized? This place does not exist in a particular area that you can point to or that you can see. It actually exists within the pure perceptions. An entire buddhafield could exist in one speck of dust. The role of the teacher differs not because the teachers are of a better quality than the disciples but because of the different aspects of teachings. For example, if the teachings are vajra, the vajra buddha would appear as the main teacher. If they were padma, then the padma buddha would appear, and so on. But all are of completely equal quality. It is not that others don't have what the main one has. This is more or less the self-achievement of complete realization of emptiness and the inexhaustible fruition of the complete purification of one's true awareness of emptiness nature. It is also the fruition of infinite, inexhaustible merit that one has accumulated in one's path.

The dharmakaya is the place of undivided, superior pervasiveness where everything originates, remains, and ceases. The sambhogakaya realm never ceases, but it also arises from dharmakaya. So, we make offerings of these three kayas to the guru and lineage refuge objects in order to perfect those qualities and to accumulate merit to attain such profound, glorious qualities. This is also the training of *shinjang* of mind to open and to see more than it could see before, and to perfect the pure perception.

In the Nyingtik ngöndro, a chöd practice follows the mandala offering practice. From beginningless time, ignorance has caused beings to grasp at an ego that ultimately doesn't exist. Our ego grasps to this "I," which is nonexistent and can't be found in any part of our body. Realizing this very clearly, offer your body. Because we grasp this *I*, we have a lot of negative emotions that arise, and taking action based on those negative emotions, we create karma for further suffering. But if you really look carefully, there is no such thing as *I*. If you examine all the parts of your body trying to find this *I*, you realize you can't find the body itself, either. For example, if you take your hand apart into pieces—i.e., this right index finger, this pinky—you won't find a "hand." By examining in this way, you come to the conclusion that you can't find anything, yet we grasp to these things as solid and substantial, as when we say, "My body. I am."

So now it's time to give up on these kinds of ideas. Offer your body to the Three Precious Jewels, and offer your body to all the demons, or whoever is there to take your body, whoever has the connection or karma to be obstacles to your body or your mind. Just naturally give it up. Give up protecting your body and mind. If you do this chöd practice, you will realize that there is no such thing as *I*, even though we cling to an *I*. There is no such thing as a body, yet we cling to a body. Due to this clinging, we have developed a lot of attachment and hatred. Give up this attachment to *I* and body. Instead, take this body to be like a magician's form, and offer it to the Three Precious Jewels, the demons, or whoever has any karma to be an obstacle to your body and mind, and then dedicate your prayer to make it clear.

In the Nyingtik ngöndro, the chöd practice begins when you say "PHET!" You then transfer through the crown of your head your consciousness, which turns into black Thröma, who holds in one hand a skullcup and in her other, a knife. Thröma cuts off the top of your skull with the knife, and your skull becomes unimaginably big. Then Thröma cuts off all the parts of your body and puts them in the skullcup. OM purifies; AH transforms, making it dutsi; and HUNG makes it into any imaginable thing. You offer it all to the nirmanakaya, sambhogakaya, and dharmakaya buddhalands and give the rest to the demons and devils. That is the practice being spoken about here. When you perform this chöd practice, you accumulate the same merit as if you were to give up your real body. It creates a very good habit of giving rather than protecting yourself.

We have to talk about ego. Egotistical grasping thinks that an ego exists and that this ego is permanent, singular, and independent. When we examine, we see that ego doesn't exist in the body, speech, or mind. Understanding that the body, speech, and mind—those things we take to be "me," "I," or "ego"—are not permanent, singular, or independent, we see that ego does not really exist. The egotistical mind is more or less an illusion. Nonetheless, this ego tendency has tremendous care for and attachment to body, speech, and mind, and especially to the body because it is more substantial and has been so carefully protected from harm. By protecting the body, many negative actions have come to fruition in our mental continuum. Realizing that, one completely gives up attachment to body and sees the body as empty.

Through ego, we become involved with negative emotions and have created negative actions. Realizing that we are completely attached to our body, we can turn that self-care into caring for others by visualizing the body as empty and making offerings of amrita to all the demons and other sentient beings who have a karmic debt with us, inviting them as our kind guests, and making offerings to them of the amrita. With the complete conviction that ego grasping and its clinging to the body as real are the source of suffering, one knows that letting go of that grasping is the only way to achieve freedom from suffering and demonic sources. Sentient beings are a great help for that, and you can really let go of attachment to your physical body and perfectly do the visualization. Then all the obstacles can be overcome and turned into enrichment for your practice.

There are two different ways of accumulating merit in ngöndro practice—mandala offerings and the yogi's feast offering, chöd. Yogis don't always have anything to feast on, so they offer their body. Because you do this visualization practice, or any visualization practice—but especially visualizing turning your body into amrita and making offerings—it will benefit you in the bardo. In the bardo, you follow your light body while thinking it's your real body. If you've let go of ego attachment for your body and given it out as amrita to all the sentient beings, then in the bardo, by not being attached to your body, you'll have the recognition that you're practicing. This will allow you to be able to let go of clinging to the light body and to understand the true nature of mind. You will realize your unobscured, true nature of mind.

Finally, in the guru yoga section, you unify your mind with your teacher's mind and the entire lineage of teachers going back to the Buddha himself. First there is the guru outside, from whom you receive teachings. Your practice of guru yoga is to properly receive teachings and to turn your mind toward the Dharma, to become a dharmic person. Secondly, your own insight, studies, and contemplations contribute to your having the correct view. And thirdly, you realize your own mind as inseparable from the guru's mind. This is important for self-liberation—all thoughts dissolving into emptiness. Finally, you understand that the first, second, and third guru yoga practices are all in your mind. You see it as a manifestation of the complete, undefiled wisdom of your own mind. Then the precious guru always appears in your mind with complete devotion and trust. If you don't lack devotion and trust, wherever you are in the three realms, you will receive blessings. But if you don't have this trust, devotion, and understanding of the guru yoga practice, then even if the guru were your father, it would not have any special effect. The ultimate guru is not the physical form but the enlightened mind, which is completely pervasive.

Visualizing the guru in front of you, reciting the mantras of the guru, and receiving blessings is relative guru yoga practice. Absolute guru yoga practice is sustaining the awareness that is inseparable from the guru's mind. And with the complete guru yoga practice, you could nurture your enlightened seed into complete fruition by the gracious blessings of the guru. Having the guru's blessings is the only way to achieve enlightenment. There's no second way for that.

In guru yoga practice, the embodiment of all the buddhas is your own root guru. Your guru holds all the lineages and is the embodiment of all the deities, dakinis, and protectors. Your teacher thus contains vast blessings. You pray to your teacher, visualizing your guru on top of your head during the day and in your heart at night. Doing the practice of guru yoga and visualizing your guru on top of your head or in your heart creates the same merit as if you were visualizing all the buddhas and receiving the blessings of all the deities, dakinis, protectors, and the Three Precious Jewels.

Guru yoga is the most important practice for gaining enlightenment. The most important thing during guru yoga practice is to rest in the true nature of mind, which is a great benefit for your path. At the end of guru yoga practice, you take the three initiations from your guru's body, speech, and mind. The OM, AH, and HUNG come into your forehead, throat, and heart to bestow upon you the qualities of the Buddha's body, speech, and mind.

To practice guru yoga, visualize the guru in front of you as the embodiment of all the buddhas and bodhisattvas. The guru's nature and the Buddha's nature are inseparable. There is only one nature. Your nature, the guru's nature, and the Buddha's nature are inseparable. We do this practice of guru yoga in order to realize the guru's nature, which is our nature that has been hidden from us. So, visualize the guru in front of you, on a lotus, in the form of Padmasambhava, his nature the same as that of your own root guru's. Then you recite the mantra.

The most important thing about this practice is not visualizing the guru and reciting the mantra but understanding that your guru's mind, your mind, and everyone's mind, is one nature. The nature is enlightenment. The nature is the true, complete state of dharmakaya, sambhogakaya, and nirmanakaya. So, it is important to remain in that, which is called "mixing the mind of the guru with your mind." But it isn't like mixing two separate things, like water and milk. *Mixing* means remaining in your natural state of mind, and in whatever arises, liberating the thoughts. If you can liberate whatever thoughts arise, they become wisdom, perfection, and they are no longer kleshas. Even if they appear as anger, desire, or jealousy, if you don't lose the essence of that and can remain in the essence and see it arising in that state of mind, that becomes wisdom. It is a manifestation of your natural mind, like the radiating rays of the sun.

If you have that understanding, then whatever you see, hear, or think will be inseparable from your guru's form, your guru's speech, and your guru's mind. In that way, there is no such thing as a guru outside yourself. The guru is within you. Also, there is no such thing as going somewhere, getting somewhere, or waiting to go somewhere. With this understanding, wherever you are, whoever you are, there is nothing wrong with that. Everything turns into the field of sambhogakaya and nirmanakaya, and into the activities of sambhogakaya and nirmanakaya.

For instance, when the Buddha was alive, there was one teacher, a bodhisattva who came from a pure land and received the Buddha's blessing. One day he and Shariputra were having a discussion. Shariputra said, "I see this world as it is, with all of its suffering, negativity, and negative appearances." The bodhisattva said, "I see this place completely as a pure land, with no negativities and no kleshas." Then, all of a sudden, the Buddha showed up and turned the place into a sambhogakaya pure land. The Buddha said there are different perspectives. Nothing really exists outside; it is all within your mind and your own perception. If you perfect the true nature of mind, you will see everything as deity, hear everything as mantra, and perceive everything as wisdom. If you don't have that view, that quality of practice, what you see will be negative, what you hear will be negative, and what you perceive will be negative.

So there really is nothing outside. Everything is within your own mind. It depends on how you handle your mind.

This is not like working very hard to have good thoughts and to avoid bad thoughts. Increasing one's good thoughts and exhausting one's bad thoughts involve effort, pressure, and force, and this creates something that is impermanent. Anything impermanent is suffering. Just perfecting and realizing your own view clearly changes the whole perspective of your hearing, seeing, and perceiving.

There is no such thing as changing places, like going to a pure land. There is no such thing as really hearing the mantra sound all the time. There is no such thing as just vanishing into some state of mind with no thoughts. What I am saying is that the most important thing is your point of view, how you perfect your point of view. It takes time to perfect your view, a lot of time and skill. But perfecting your view has nothing to do with pressure and hard work. It involves understanding and seeing very clearly and naturally. Pressure is grasping, and grasping never works in practice anyway.

If you have a good teacher who knows how to teach very well, someone with experience who can teach you how to perfect the right view, who can introduce your mind to you and help you to clearly see your suffering mind, then when you examine your mind, more and more, you will see it has no substance and that there is nothing to hold onto. Mind has no shape, no color, and no form. You will see thoughts coming up, one after another, and within a thought there is space, which you can sometimes experience, but rarely. Then you will learn how to relax in that space. This space we are speaking of is indescribable. It seems illogical that something is called indescribable, but it is because it is beyond the conceptual mind.

As you continue to examine your mind, you will realize that within this space, all thoughts arise and dissolve, but when the thoughts arise, the space does not disappear; it is always there. Space contains the thoughts. Then you will see thoughts very clearly, without defilements, even if the thought is an angry one. When you remain in that view, every thought turns into wisdom and doesn't cause any negative actions. More and more, you will discover the true nature of your mind, and when that becomes stable, you will see thoughts arising and dissolving in that nature. So, thoughts are no longer such a big deal, though of course, in some sense, thoughts are a big deal since they are used to communicate and describe your emotions and preferences. These kinds of thoughts are very important in this world. But you cannot cling to these thoughts of liking and not liking, enjoying and not enjoying. Since that is the way the world is, practitioners will express themselves in that way too, but without clinging. Then you completely turn ignorance into awareness, kleshas into wisdom, and you become enlightened, even though you don't have the form of Buddha.

Part Three

The bees received many teachings and tried to practice them, but they were still attached to their own phenomena and luxuries. Time passed.

One day, the female bee, Ngakyen, was enjoying herself while drinking sweet nectar from a flower. The male bee, Dabyang, was flying around basking in the sun and the fragrant blossoms. But after a few minutes, the rays of the sun disappeared. The shadow of a black cloud fell upon the earth, and all the petals of all the flowers closed at one time. Ngakyen was trapped in one of them. She was frightened and could hardly breathe. All she could say was, "Buzz, buzz, buzz."

When Dabyang realized what had happened to Ngakyen, he felt helpless and afraid. He fell to the ground, crying. Rolling around in anguish, he cried out:

How frightening and scary! What evil circumstances!
What will happen to us? Who caused this evil?
Who has the power to dominate the brightness of the sun?
Who has the power to close the petals of the flowers?
Where has my dear heart gone?
Where has my beautiful Ngakyen gone?

Where has my beautiful singer gone?
Where has my kind-hearted friend gone?
Where is the beautiful one who flies?
Where has my dear piece of heart gone?
Please don't leave my chest empty!
Get up, get up, please! Don't you hear me?
If you don't reply, my heart will break into a thousand pieces.
You hard-hearted cloud. Why have you picked us to harm?
Kind flower! Don't you have the power to open up?
Compassionate sun, please don't sit behind the clouds!
Come out and shine on us.
If I were the wind, what great joy I would feel
to blow away this harmful cloud.
If I were a man, I would open the flowers.
Isn't there anyone to help this cloud go away?
Ngakyen, Ngakyen, my heart, Ngakyen!
Where are you, where are you? Can't you hear me?

Ngakyen could only faintly raise her voice, calling:
"Dabyang, Dabyang."

Hearing her, Dabyang was happy to know that Ngakyen
was still alive. He got up excitedly and called her name,
touching his head to the flower.

Ngakyen could hear his voice, and she thought:

Ah ka ka. When we went to see the teacher,
we received many teachings but did little practice.
We promised to practice, but our life continued as usual,
and we only imagined practicing in the future.
Now I'm trapped in a flower, and I must suffer and die.
Perhaps the sun will shine on us and loosen the petals
to free me.
But now Dabyang is sad, and I must say something to him.

So Ngakyen called out to Dabyang:

Kyé, kyé! Dabyang, my friend, son of the goddess,
I'm so happy to hear your voice, but
I'm sad that I can't see your beautiful face.
What misfortune caused this suffering to occur?
I could never have imagined that death could come so suddenly.
Where is the kind-hearted sun?
I would never have imagined that
a beautiful flower with such sweet nectar,
scent, and color could become a cause for my death.
The petals have become the bars of my prison,
the nectar the rope around my neck.

What sorrow I feel.
When we listened to the teachings,
we heard of the impermanence of samsara.
Today, I realize this so well.

Our wealth could have competed with a goddess's,
but in the blink of an eye, I am on the brink of death.

I had a mind to do the noble practice
but no courage to practice it.
Now when I must make the journey to the bardo,
I have nothing to rely on.
Even though I knew samsara was full of suffering,
I was unable to cut my attachments
to the pleasures of the five perceptions.
Now, the attachment to these pleasures
has become the source of my suffering.
I have some understanding of the cause and effect of karma
but have been unable to abandon negative actions
or increase positive actions.

When I review my life, I see little merit.
I never thought of leaving the soft cushion of these flower petals,
but today I'm being led to the door of death.
I never thought of leaving these delicious nectars,
but now, against my will, I must go to the bardo,
where I can only enjoy the scent.
I never thought of being separated from my parents,
but now death is taking me to the bardo,
where I have no relatives.
I never thought of leaving my children,
but now death is taking me to the bardo.
Death is pushing me to the bardo,
the long, lonely journey to rebirth.
I never thought of leaving my velvet coat,
but now death is taking me to the bardo.
I never thought of losing my dear friend,
Dabyang, Golden Bee,
but now death is taking me to the bardo,
where I cannot hear or see him.

Kyé, kyé, my dear heart friend.
Since we met, you've always been so kind and bright.
I've never experienced any darkness in you.
You've only shown me kind words and have
never scolded me.
You've only shown me love.
I cannot remember you not being loving to me.
Among our wealth, there has never been a word like
mine or *yours*.
During our lifetime, you have never looked down
upon my actions.
The kindness you have shown me will always be in my heart.
The loving words you have shared with me will always
be in my heart.
The stability of your companionship will always be in my heart.
It seems I must leave this place,
but I have no attachment to it.
I must leave my wealth, but I have no attachment to it.
I must leave my servants here,
but I have no attachment to their services.
I must leave my body, but I have no attachment to this flesh.
It seems my life is ended here, but I have
no attachment to it.
But to leave you, my dear friend Dabyang,
and your loving kindness, I cannot bear.
Over this, I cannot control my tears.
Remembering your kindness, my mind is filled with sorrow.
Remembering your speech,
my heart is filled with the fires of sorrow.
Now the time of karma has come.
What can we do to prevent it?
The nature of suffering is upon me.
Who can prevent it?
Please think about this situation.
Please remember our promise, and practice the Dharma.

And Dabyang replied:

Kyé, kyé, Ngakyen.
Oh, Ngakyen, the singer, my turquoise bee.
Don't be frightened! Have confidence!
The fear of suffering is temporary.
This cloud will not remain for long.
There must be a way to solve this problem.
If we use our wealth properly, we can clear away this obstacle.
There must be a method for dispelling this storm.
If we ask the advice of knowledgeable beings,
they will surely have an answer.
If we take refuge in powerful beings,
perhaps everything will be fine.

The black crows who give predictions
live throughout the villages and rocky mountains.
If we approach them, they could give us predictions.
On the high roof beams, there are many gatherings
of sparrows reciting mantras of great benefit.
If we invite them, they can come to our home and recite mantras.
In the deep pond lives an ugly, flat-faced frog
who is a messenger of the nagas.
If we make a request for his help,
he may have a method for solving this problem.
He could help us.

In the jungle dwells a poisonous snake.
He is the form of the water element.
If we take refuge in him, the clouds will surely clear!
In their holes in the hills and high mountains sit the gophers,
dedicated retreatants with great powers of meditation.
They can work wonders!
On the branches of trees perch the cuckoo birds,
the lords of clouds and rain.
If we please them, they will stop the rain.

In the mountain meadows many wild burros graze.
When they lift their jeweled mouths to the sky,
they call forth the sun.
The great killer of beings—the spider—creeps
in unexpected places.
As he is a manifestation of a naga himself, if we please him,
he will help us.
In the crevices of the mountain live black bats.
They are messengers of the garuda.
Perhaps they can stop such evil.

There are no obstacles that cannot be overcome,
no negativities that cannot be purified,
no suffering that cannot be uprooted.
We will find a solution.

With this in mind, Dabyang set off for an answer. He met
with a crow, who said:

Though it is caused by the naga and can be solved by a garuda,
the circumstances necessary to resolve the problem
have to do with the wind.
The situation is bad at present but ultimately will be okay.

Next, he spoke with the leader of the sparrows, who said:

The blessings of the gathering sparrows are like fire.
If it can burn the whole forest, why not a small patch of grass?
But, of course, meanwhile, you must serve us well,
and the offering must be good!

Then they all did mantras. Afterward, Dabyang went to
see the frog in the deep, dark pond. The frog told him:

I'm the frog who faces great danger.
I'm the messenger of the nagas.

The clouds came from the ocean.
If we ask the nagas to resolve the problem, it will be okay.

He looked at the sky and went "ting-ting" with his eyebrows.

Following this conversation, he met with a
poisonous snake, who hissed:

The oneness of the water element made the clouds and hail.
Only I, the snake, have the power to control this! No problem.

With that, he wound into a coil.

Later, Dabyang found a gopher in his hole, sitting in
meditation. He told the gopher the problem, and he answered:

I meditate without distraction, but I cannot let you down.
In between my meditations, I will do rituals for you.
Ultimately, this problem will completely pass.

With that, he blinked his eyes.

Dabyang consulted with the cuckoo bird on a high
branch. The bird said:

The rain is blessed by heavens' command,
and I am her earthly messenger.
I have little power to control the rain.

With that, the bird cocked his head.

He consulted the wild burro next, who told him:

I, the wild burro, have been blessed with the
jewel of the mouth.
I have the power to clear any obstacles.

You were smart to come see me.
I will definitely solve your problem.

With that he lifted his mouth to the sky.

Dabyang found a spider in an unexpected place,
and the spider told him:

Clouds are the breath of the spider.
They can only be cleared up by my kind.
If you bring meat to my net,
I will solve this problem.

As he spoke, he spun a web.

At last, Dabyang met with the head of the hawk clan, who replied:

The nagas are my prey.
I will absolutely make them pay for what they are doing to you.
Meanwhile, don't you worry. I'll solve this one for you.

Dabyang thought optimistically:

All these great animals say everything will ultimately be fine.
The flower will soon blossom, and Ngakyen will be free.

He relaxed quietly.

All of a sudden, a black cloud spun from the four directions.
From the east came the thunder of the dragon. As the wind
blew, the flowers tightened. Ngakyen's legs and arms were
crushed, and she could hardly breathe. She spoke to Dabyang
in a very soft voice.

Kyé, kyé, Dabyang, son of the goddess.
The flower is tightening; the nectar is surrounding me,

and the petals are closing in.
I can hardly move, breathe, or speak. I am suffocating.
Now I have no chance to escape.
The thunder of the dragon resounds from all directions.
The wind is blowing. The flowers are tightening.
I'm sure it will hail.

When the storm comes, it will flatten the grass
and cut the blooming flowers from their stems.
It will be as if the earth and the sky had reversed.
It will be as if mountains were crumbling.
Great trees will bend.
You also must leave at once, as I will not be freed.
But before we separate, I must say a few important words.

The teachings are now clear in my mind.
I have been introduced to the nature of suffering.
The nature of gathering is that it separates.
Have you seen the nature of suffering?
Have you renounced the suffering and realized
the uncertainty of death?
Do you see the tricks of the five perceptions?

Even though I've seen a noble teacher,
I regret that I didn't study more.
Even though I was taught to practice,
I regret that I didn't sit.
Even though I have a fortunate birth,
I regret that I didn't learn the essence of giving.
Even though I knew death would come,
I regret that I didn't prepare.
Even though I have heard of the cause and effect of karma,
I regret that 1 didn't practice well.

Now death has come unexpectedly.
The darkness of death is before my eyes.

I'm afraid I won't see clearly.
The wind of karma is pushing me forward.
I'm afraid of no control.
Scary sounds fill my ears.
I'm afraid of bardo appearances.
The rope of death is around my neck.
The evil of death is dragging me forward.
I'm afraid of loneliness.
I'm afraid of unknown destinations.
Oh, the sufferings of samsara are so many,
like the stars in the sky.

Dabyang, go practice! Don't delay.
Please abandon any thoughts of life's pleasures
as though they were poison.
Life should become practice.
Become accomplished in your practice,
and show me the path.
Now go before the hail falls!
I pray you remain for a long time
to accomplish Dharma and fulfill your wishes.

As these words were spoken, Ngakyen was suffocating.
Dabyang's heart felt as if it had been pierced by a thorn. His
mind was filled with sorrow, and he said, "Ah, ka, ka."

The rain began to fall, and hail covered the earth. Dabyang
left helplessly and hid in a hole in the field. The earth became
white with hailstones. The rivers were churning, and the storm was
washing away the soil. The plants were crushed, flattened under
the hail, and the stems of the grass and flowers were cut down.

Commentary on Part Three
The bees received many teachings and tried to practice them,
but they were still attached to their own phenomena and
luxuries. They were moved and inspired to try to practice as

much as they could, but because they were still attached to their own lives, they carried on with life as usual.

All of us experience this. Even when we have some insight into the impermanent and shifty nature of our world and some idea about where clinging to such things leads, nevertheless, our habits are very strong. Beyond that, even when we've heard Dharma teachings and have a glimpse of the possibility of liberation and how to attain it, still, this glimpse and inspiration do not of their own accord alter the strength of our habits of clinging to worldly, samsaric phenomena. For as long as we have known, we have been attached not simply to the pleasures of worldly things but to the sense of confirmation they provide in our belief in ourselves. This isn't particularly philosophical. We just act as if we're going along, and the world around us will continue to support that. To develop genuine renunciation and cultivate compassion means to overcome our habits almost on the level of neurological reactions. And to do that takes a lot of practice.

The important thing to realize when you hear this story is that you get so involved in samsara that you don't see what can happen to you. Before you know it, a situation happens that you have no control over, and you just panic; you can't help yourself. But since we have all heard and practiced the Dharma, we still have time to practice and become enlightened so that we don't have regrets when it's time to die.

This is exactly what happens to the bees. A terrible storm suddenly arises, and the chill that it brings causes all the flower blossoms to tightly close. Ngakyen, the female bee, is trapped in one, and, as you may remember, she sings: "What misfortune caused this suffering to occur? I could never have imagined that death could come so suddenly."

Once, just before winter, Milarepa decided to go for retreat into the mountains. His disciples and friends told him not to go because the mountains were very high and would get lots of snow, so he might not be able to get out. At that time, Milarepa wasn't able to fly. He made his way up there, and it snowed for a very long time. In the beginning, Milarepa saw some obstacles, but he made friends with the local spirits and didn't have problems with the others. Eventually, he could sit in the snow by practicing tummo, so he stayed there for the whole winter.

At the end of winter, his disciples and friends thought he surely must be dead because they thought there was no way he could have survived up there in that heavy snow. They thought, "If only he had listened to us, he would be alive now." Later, when the snow started to melt, they made a big feast and burned a lot of food outside. On that same day, Milarepa was very hungry, but he still couldn't get out of that area because of the snow, so when the food was burned outside, he sensed something very interesting. His stomach felt full, and he felt invigorated.

Finally, his friends were able to go up to look for his body. When Milarepa met them, he asked, "On such and such a day, what did you do?" And they said, "Oh, we thought you were dead, so we made a big soup for you." Then he told them, "Yes, I sensed that. I was feeling very good, as was my stomach." This is why when someone dies, a lot of food is burned outside and prayers are offered because bardo beings can only "eat" the scent. So, I think it's true that bardo beings are able to sense and feel through their stomachs better than we can. They don't have a rough body like ours, but they have this extremely acute sense of smell. As Ngakyen said, "I never thought of leaving these delicious nectars, but now, against my will, I must go to the bardo, where I can only enjoy the scent. I never thought of being separated from my parents, but now death is taking me to the bardo, where I have no relatives."

I chose to teach on this story because it cuts through all the bullshit. Actually, all of Patrul Rinpoche's songs and teachings always have something to say about politics and bullshit. He also comments on a lot of Tibetan rituals in this story when Dabyang tells Ngakyen not to be frightened because there must be a method for clearing away the clouds. He wonders whether asking the advice "of knowledgeable beings" might help and considers asking a frog "who is a messenger of the nagas." A naga is a kind of spirit that lives under the water. Its upper body is human, and its lower body is like a snake. There are male and female nagas, and they can be harmful to beings, though there are good and bad nagas.

This section portrays many Tibetan beliefs or myths, such as the belief that frogs are messengers of nagas, and that the spider is a manifestation of a naga. They believe that when the cuckoo bird stops singing, it means rain won't come. Cuckoo birds are present only in the rainy season. Thus, in the winter, there is no song of the cuckoo birds and no rain. Burros are supposed to have the power to bring the sun by using their mouth. When it's really snowy and cold, and sun would be welcome, Tibetans believe that wild burros get together and do this thing with their mouths that makes the sun come out. They also believe that the snake is the spirit of the waters, and since clouds form from water, a snake can make it rain. These are Tibetan cultural beliefs.

In the same way as described here, Tashi Gelek, the man whose wife was sick, visited many ritual people and ngakpas, different people who did divinations, or *mos,* and various other rituals to try to heal his wife. So Patrul Rinpoche uses all of these animals to represent the people that the man consulted when his wife had smallpox. Similarly, Golden Bee visits different animals to consult with them in the hope that they might help his mate, the turquoise bee, who is trapped in a flower. These animals have a lot to say because they really think they're positive beings. This would be like someone in this culture going around to visit many new age psychics for advice.

In Tibet, the first thing people do when someone is sick is to get a *mo* or divination from a lama. This usually costs money, and they will also tell you to do various rituals to help. Then they do these rituals and bring in all the monks to do a lot of pujas and put out a lot of things. Sometimes it helps, of course. But even though these things help, they're only temporary. They might help you to solve a particular problem or extend your life for another five or six years, but they won't give you enlightenment.

So, Dabyang went to see all of these beings, first meeting with a crow who said, "Though it is caused by the naga and can be solved by a garuda, the circumstances necessary to resolve the problem have to do with the wind. The situation is bad at present but ultimately will be okay." Crows are supposed to be able to predict the future and to be clairvoyant.

Next Dabyang spoke with the leader of the sparrows. In Tibet, people bring a lot of monks into their homes to do rituals and recite certain mantras, so here, sparrows are supposed to be the monks. Dabyang spoke to their leader, who said, "The blessings of the gathering sparrows are like fire. If it can burn the whole forest, why not a small patch of grass?" Dabyang's problem is likened to a small patch of grass. "But, of course, meanwhile you must serve us well, and the offerings must be good!"

Then Dabyang went to see the frog who was living in the pond, and the frog said, "I'm the frog who faces great danger. I'm the messenger of the nagas. The clouds came from the ocean. If we ask the nagas to resolve the problem, it will be okay." Because the nagas live in the ocean, which makes clouds, and the frog came from the ocean too, the frog is the messenger of the nagas. Now that he came to the frog to ask for help, the frog looked at the sky with a funny expression— and you know how people's faces can make funny expressions. In Tibet, if you do that, it's a sign that you're fooling around.

Dabyang began to feel optimistic after going to see all of these animals. They all sounded very positive, and all of these powerful and very well-known beings said that ultimately this was not going to be a problem, so Ngakyen might be set free. Dabyang started to relax a bit, and he breathed a sigh of relief and sat quietly for some time.

Then, he saw these huge, black clouds gathering from the four directions beginning to take dramatic shapes. The sound of thunder came from the east, louder and louder, with lightning flashing all around. Wind was furiously blowing— shoo, shoo, shoo—and big drops of hail fell. The flowers started

170

shaking, so Dabyang flew to Ngakyen's flower where she was calling Dabyang's name. Then Ngakyen said her last words to him: "The teachings are now clear in my mind. I have been introduced to the nature of suffering. The nature of gathering is that it separates. Have you seen the nature of suffering?" The teacher said that the nature of gathering is separating and that ultimately everyone would suffer, that everyone would go away. Dabyang and Ngakyen knew that, but they hadn't taken it seriously. Now Ngakyen clearly realizes that everything in samsara is suffering, although previously it had seemed that there were a lot of pleasures. Now everything that had been pleasure was turning into suffering.

Ngakyen continues, "Have you renounced the suffering and realized the uncertainty of death?" The teacher told them that death was uncertain and could come at any time, that you never knew when death would come, but they'd always thought they would live a long time. Now, all of a sudden, they realize that death would not come tomorrow but was happening now.

Ngakyen asks, "Do you see the tricks of the five perceptions?" What she means is that our minds are tricked by the objects of the five perceptions—form, sensation, hearing, smelling, and tasting. By being so attached to them, we create a lot of negativity and karma. By indulging in such temporary pleasures and luxuries, we aren't able to complete the Dharma and do the practice. This is why we don't practice.

"Even though I've seen a noble teacher, I regret I didn't study more. Even though I was taught to practice, I regret that I didn't sit." They received a lot of teachings but just listened to them, and though the teachings made them feel different at the time, they didn't really practice enough to accomplish the practice. Now Ngakyen regrets that she didn't sit enough. "Even though I have a fortunate birth, I regret that I didn't learn the essence of giving." She had a precious body, but she didn't use it because she didn't practice.

If you practice, then your body and your life become precious; otherwise, you don't accomplish anything. "Even though I knew death would come, I regret that I didn't prepare," Ngakyen says. Even though she knew that death would come one day, if she had done the practice, she would have accomplished something that would have prepared her to accept her death. But because she didn't prepare, she feels such regret in her heart.

Although we can read this story, it can be tricky for us. We know that death can strike us at any time, but because we're in samsara and attached to all our present pleasures and luxuries, we're unable to realize that truth and develop a strong feeling of determination to really sit and do the practice. But when death comes, it's too late.

"Even though I have heard of the cause and effect of karma, I regret that I didn't practice well. Now death has come unexpectedly. The darkness of death is before my eyes." Death is close to Ngakyen. Just before someone dies, their perceptions close, and it becomes completely dark. But one who has the practice never loses the clarity of the true nature of mind, and there is never a darkening; therefore, the practitioner doesn't panic in this darkness. But Ngakyen doesn't have the practice or the clarity of her own mind, so this darkening occurs right in front of her eyes.

"The wind of karma is pushing me forward," Ngakyen says. The reason death comes is due to the force of karma. You don't die for no reason. Karma is like the wind pushing you toward death. "I'm afraid of no control," she says. When you die, you have no control. The wind just pushes you forward. "Scary sounds fill my ears," she continues. "I'm afraid of bardo appearances." When you die, a lot of appearances come up in your mind. They are not visual appearances, like those we see with our perceptions; they are in our mind. It's true that many appearances come up in the bardo, some wrathful. In Tibet, there are many hunters who hunt every day, who just before they die experience the pain of that, crying, "Oh please, take this away. Chase this animal away! This animal is poking at me and stepping on me!" There are many stories about hunters saying these kinds of things before they die.

Ngakyen cries, "The rope of death is around my neck. The evil of death is dragging me forward. I'm afraid of loneliness. I'm afraid of unknown destinations." She knows she's dying, but she doesn't know where she's going. It's very scary to not know where you're going. Even in an ordinary way, going to an unknown place can be a very scary and lonely experience. But this is not just an ordinary place—this is death.

Finally, Ngakyen tells Dabyang to practice without delay and not to think he'll be able to practice tomorrow. Just do it. Also, if anybody gives him advice for this life's pleasures, don't take it. It's all bullshit because everything is going to end this way. Everybody has to face death, and if you take their advice and get more engaged in this life, if you get more distracted from your practice, you may miss the chance to practice. So, any advice for this life should be abandoned like poison. Don't take it.

Ngakyen began to suffocate. The rain became intense and the thunder and lightning more dramatic. It began to hail, and all of a sudden Dabyang couldn't stay there any longer. Feeling very sad, his heart burning like fire and as if poked by a thorn, he flew away, trying to escape with his broken heart and tears streaming from his eyes. The weather became more and more dramatic, and the taller flowers were cut off, the shorter ones were smashed, and trees bent to the ground. The fields were completely flooded, and the beautiful grass on the hills was washed away. Then the thunder, the sound of the dragon, got louder and louder, and the lightening became more and more dramatic. Once in a completely peaceful, quiet, and enjoyable place, now Ngakyen was caught suffocating in a flower.

This teaching is meant to make us realize that the time of death is uncertain, and that we shouldn't get caught up in life's temporary pleasures. If we're looking for pleasure, we should look for the ultimate pleasure, enlightenment, and realize that samsara is a place of natural suffering. Don't delay your practice. Don't get to the point where you regret that you received teachings, that you had a practice but didn't really accomplish the practice. Don't think that you'll be able to practice tomorrow, or the day after tomorrow, or next week. Death can come at any time. In fact, today there are more circumstances for death in this world than ever before. Disease and fighting cause death, as do many modern technologies, like cars, electricity, taking the wrong medicine, and readily available weapons. So, this teaching is to make you realize that death is certain and that you should not delay your practice. You should be completely dedicated to your practice.

All of us here are Dharma practitioners, but this doesn't mean we're trying to "save face" or to have a certain image of ourselves. A Dharma practitioner is someone who has confidence that they'll become enlightened in this lifetime. It's very important to try your best to become enlightened in this lifetime, and if that doesn't work, to have confidence that you'll be enlightened in the bardo. If not in the bardo, then have a confident, clear understanding that you have enough positive actions to be reborn in a place where there is Dharma, in order to be able to practice and attain enlightenment.

These three confidences are very important. Without them, you're bullshitting, and any practice you may do is just temporary and only for this life. If you only practice to calm your mind, to relax or whatever, it's bullshit. If you're really diligent, then you'll have confidence that you'll attain enlightenment in this lifetime. However, if you see that you really can't, then you'll definitely feel confident that you'll attain enlightenment in the bardo. Even in the bardo, if you're convinced of karma and never bullshit when it comes to action and merit, you'll definitely have a clear mind that you will take a positive rebirth in your next lifetime.

It's important to know that death is always individual. When someone dies, one always gets completely caught up in one's own world. But in this society, we pressure the dying not to get caught up in their own world. We want them to make a will, to say this and that. Many people will follow those kinds of rules. With Ngakyen, the sweetness of the flower became the sticky and tight rope around her neck. Death is always individual, no matter where you are. As Milarepa sang:

No one to ask me if I'm sick,
No one to mourn me when I die:
To die here alone in this hermitage
Is everything a yogi could wish for.

No trace of feet outside my door
No trace of blood within:
To die here alone in this hermitage
Is everything a yogi could wish for.

No one to wonder where I've gone,
No particular place to go.
To die here alone in this hermitage
Is everything a yogi could wish for.

My corpse can rot and be eaten by worms,
My gristle and bone be sucked dry by flies;
To die here alone in this hermitage
Is everything a yogi could wish for.

He sang this song because death is individual. No matter
where you are, it is individual. Practitioners who have complete
confidence in practice, when they go through the bardo,
will know how to face its stages and what their destination
is. They will be very prepared. As a matter of fact, they are
waiting for that. That is why Machik Labdrön's husband and
guru, Padampa Sangye, said in a song about death, "You are
always welcome, death; I invite you any time." Because he
was prepared, he could take it very coolly. There are definitely
advantages to doing this practice. Milarepa also said, "I was
scared of death when I went to the mountains, and I thought of
impermanence all the time. Now I am free of the fear of death,
and death is always welcome." For these people, death is the
same as being born, the same as any experience. In fact, if one is
not completely accomplished, death helps a lot. It brings many
advantages because there is no gross body to interfere.

Part Four

Dabyang's heart was full of sorrow. Tears fell from his eyes. He sat helplessly as the sun emerged from the clouds. Soon the flowers began to blossom. Dabyang watched the happy expressions of the other bees. He noticed that all the things that once brought him joy now only saddened him.

Dabyang began to sing of renunciation:

Kyé-hu, kyé-hu, kyé-hu.
What sorrow, what sorrow, what sorrow.
This is the condition of samsara.
Everything is like a magician's display:
See how illusory and impermanent it is.
Everything is the mind's fabrication:
See how easily it all unravels and falls apart.
How beguiling the pleasures are:
See how quickly they desert you.
All the petals of the flowers have been cut by the hail.
All the fresh, green shoots have fallen upon the earth.
The valley that seemed so cheerful this morning is
now filled with sorrow;
the body and spirit of my dearest companion have
now separated.

Now I, Dabyang, who once possessed great ambition
and confidence, have lost all hope.
All that previously made me happy fills me with sorrow.
What was this morning a beautiful six-legged being
is now lifeless matter.
As I think of this situation, my mind is filled with pain.
Any brightness in me is smothered. What sadness!

How sudden this Devil-Death came to my dear Ngakyen.
I wonder when he will visit me.
I pray to my guru. I pray to my guru.

Poor Dabyang, poor Dabyang.
Turn my mind to the Dharma!
Bless me, my guru! Bless me, my guru!

As he sang, he felt compelled to leave the garden and found himself flying toward the mountain where the guru dwelled. He sang the song of the yogis, the happiest of all beings:

All you beautiful flowers—you only bring me sadness.
All five objects of the five perceptions—you only cause suffering.
My dear heart, lifetime companion—
your lifeless form brings me sadness.
I pray to the Three Jewels: Let me practice only Dharma.
What is the point of building if buildings eventually crumble?
What is the point of accumulating if everything is impermanent?
What is the point of gathering if we all must separate?
What is the point of climbing to power when one
must eventually fall?
What is the point of attachment to one's life
if one must eventually die?

By now, my dear karmically-linked companion
must be suffering in the bardo.
Nothing can help when one dies but confidence
in the practice.
Even if one possesses great wealth, death cannot be bought off.
Even if one has many retainers, they cannot be brought along.
Even if one has a dear friend, this suffering cannot be shared.
Even if one is very clever, it is impossible
to manipulate oneself out of this situation.
The law of death is unchangeable.
Merely hearing the Dharma is not fruitful—one must practice.
Merely owning a piece of land does not bring forth
crops—one must cultivate it.
Merely keeping an untamed horse is not
beneficial—one must work with it.

There is nothing else—the rest of my life will be
wrapped in Dharma.

There is no need
to think of my enemies or how to battle them,
to think of my relatives or how to please them,
to think of my wealth or how to accumulate it,
to think of my superiors or how to keep face with them,
to think of my clothes or how to choose them,
to think of my food or how to prepare it,
to think of this life's pleasures.

Any attachments are obstacles.
There is no need to get attached to my thoughts,
as they are illusions.
Without fabricating thoughts, rest the mind in calmness.
Without fixating on concepts, let the mind express itself freely.
Without meditating on anything, see the true nature of mind.
Those who experience dharmakaya,
those who wander in the mountains,
the yogis, are the happiest of all beings.

Liberating illusions, few thoughts arise.
Abandoning attachments and aversions,
actions become honest.
Exhausting hope and fear, one becomes a yogi.
Without the mind's fabrications is the ordinary mind.
Without embellishing the appearance is the natural look.
Without contrived conduct or manners arises
spontaneous activity.
The yogis are the happiest of beings.

Because of one's strong courage,
one can face the hardships of practice.
Because of one's strong determination,
one can sit alone on the mountain.

Those who eat wild vegetables, the yogis,
are the happiest of beings.

One is happy if one's life goes toward Dharma.
One is sad if one is attached to this life.
One is happy alone on a mountain.
If one dwells in samsara, one suffers.
If one is attached to fame and reputation,
one becomes disappointed.
There is no end to superiors with big names,
so I will leave them where they are.
There is no end to the amount of money
I can pay my servants,
so I will leave them where they are.
There is no end to the happiness desired by my relatives,
so I will leave them where they are.
There is no end to the battle 1 can do with my enemies,
so I will leave them where they are.
There is no end to the cultivating I can do in my field,
so I will leave it where it is.
There is no end to the upkeep of my home,
so I will leave it where it is and go to the mountains.
There is no end to the delicious food I can obtain and eat,
so I will leave it to eat the wild vegetables of the mountains.
There is no end to the clothes I can buy and wear,
so I will leave them and live as a yogi.
Now I will only practice the Dharma.
Now I will only accomplish the practice.
This is my promise, victorious buddhas!

Commentary on Part Four

As the story continues, the long flowers are cut, the short
ones are squashed, and all the flowers on the ground are
completely destroyed. After it hailed, all the flowers in the
land were swept into the water, but now they've come back
up and are blooming again. The clouds are cleared away, the

sun is shining, and some bees have come out to play and sing. Dabyang just sat, his heart full of sorrow and tears running down his face. The singing bees, the beautiful flowers, the beaming sun—everything that once made him happy now made him sad with the memory of disaster. As he sat there helplessly, he sang this song: "Kyé-hu, kyé-hu, kyé-hu," which is a poetic way of expressing sorrow. "This is the condition of samsara. Everything is like a magician's display: see how illusory and impermanent it is. Everything is the mind's fabrication."

Dabyang is singing to himself, expressing his emotions and experiences, and in a way, he's very intelligent, very bright to be able to see his emotions this clearly. There is a sense that he is receiving help from the spiritual teachings he heard, even though he hasn't completely realized them because he's experiencing these emotions. Dabyang couldn't bear to stay in that place anymore, so he left.

He went to the place where he met the first guru, and as he flies around where his guru dwelled, he thought of the yogis and sang a song of how yogis are the happiest of beings. Most of these songs relate to all of our situations, but some of them may apply more to the Tibetan culture. Whatever has meaning for you, value it. If you make the images clear in your mind, the story will remain with you and help you clear up a lot of your life's confusions in samsara. It will push you to practice and guide you in your practice.

Dabyang sings about how all phenomena that are supported by perception bring only suffering, and how all the emotional states that underlie our relationship to these phenomena are futile. All attachments lead only to death, and only practice can free you from them. He is singing about renouncing those attachments. As he continues his song in this vein, he depicts the happiness of the yogi's way of life in relying solely on refuge in the Three Jewels, free from any worldly entanglements.

Part Five

At this time, a yogi named Pema Jyipa was doing retreat on the mountain. After hearing Dabyang's song, he thought:

I've heard of this golden bee, Dabyang,
whose heart is in the Dharma.
He accomplishes whatever he starts.
He's a steady being with a good character.
Motivated by certain bad circumstances,
he has achieved some renunciation.
Perhaps it is superficial and temporary.
Perhaps it's profound. Let's check and see.

The yogi approached Dabyang and said to him:

Kyé, my dear friend Golden Bee, Dabyang.
Why are you singing sad songs alone in the mountains?
It seems the unexpected devil of death has taken a rope,
tied up your dear karmic friend, and taken her away.
Please don't be so sad. Plant a piece of bone in your heart.

Pema Jyipa began testing Dabyang's commitment
to become a yogi.

The practice of worldly Dharma is a good base
for the practice of absolute Dharma.
What is the use of absolute practice without the
results of happiness?
The practice of Dharma is also for happiness.
What is the use of going for Dharma and
renouncing happiness?
You don't have to renounce everything for this.
If one friend dies, there are plenty more.
There is always a replacement.
Happiness and sadness come and go.
That's the nature of samsara.

Still, you might experience infinitely more happiness
in your life than sadness.

Certain renunciations can be the evil influences of
the demon, Radza.
Don't you know that this type of renunciation has
no substance?
Wavering devotion is the nature of the mind.
Don't you know that it has no consistency?
Sudden feelings of generosity and strong detachment
are like the hala asu tree, which bears fruit only once,
and then no more.

Renunciation can be like lightning in the sky,
which flashes but a moment and vanishes without effect.
The practice of worldly phenomena and Dharma
is the true practice of intelligence.
Don't you know such an attitude leads to the path of liberation?
Taking pleasures as the path of enlightenment
is the significance of the tantric path.
Don't you know it is the short road to enlightenment?
Remaining as king is the activity of the bodhisattva.
Don't you know its benefits?

If one is able to accumulate wealth, one can practice generosity.
Don't you know this practice contains the six prajnaparamitas?
Without being completely convinced of what one promises
to do, many conflicts and doubts arise in the mind, and one
will not end up accomplishing what one sets out to do.
Without the strength to face the difficulties of practice,
one will end up turning one's face away from the Dharma.

Without a complete understanding of renunciation, one
will desire worldly life again but find that one has
nothing left to turn to.
If one remains in a remote place without any realization,

one will become bored, and one's practice will become dull; this person will be unable to continue.

If one goes to the graveyard to practice chöd without having a good view, one will be influenced by the demons and become a servant of the devil.

If one merely acts like a siddha without possessing the qualities, one creates the circumstances for being reborn in Narak.

If one changes one's circumstances without changing one's mind, one becomes the subject of others' laughter.

If one fails to contemplate before making an important commitment, one will get caught in the cycle of regressing.

If one is not able to be steady and consistent with one's actions and projects, others won't take them seriously.

Telling others how clairvoyant you are without having the realization of emptiness distorts yourself and others.

Trying to benefit others without perfecting compassion creates attachment.

Be careful of these things.

Check clearly what comes in your mind before you feel compelled to say it.

Be mindful of your thoughts and actions,
stable and unwavering in your commitments.
Please keep this advice in your heart, Golden Bee.
This is my daily life practice.
Please don't laugh at it.
It is my secret gift to you, so please don't scold me.
If you check this out carefully, you will see for yourself.

Commentary on Part Five

From here Dabyang goes on to meet the yogi named Pema Jyipa (who is Patrul Rinpoche). In the beginning, this yogi encourages him to carry on with his life in a worldly way, telling him things like, "If one friend dies, there are plenty more," so he could really check his motivation. Dabyang would get a little upset with the yogi, who then would give him some teachings. Dabyang flew around the mountains singing sad songs. When the yogi heard Dabyang singing, he thought, "I've heard of this golden bee, Dabyang, whose heart is in the Dharma. He accomplishes whatever he starts. He's a steady being with a good character. Motivated by certain bad circumstances, he has achieved some renunciation. Perhaps it is superficial and temporary."

Because Golden Bee is in the transitional stage of renouncing his home, his family, his wealth, and his belongings to become a yogi, Pema Jyipa is making sure that he will be a good yogi and that he has some true sense of renunciation. He checks to see whether it is profound and lasting or not. Practice should not be dependent on temporary emotions, like starting to practice because one day your car won't start, and the next day when the car is fixed, you feel there's no longer any reason to practice. The wish to practice should be grounded in something more profound and based more on a view of the suffering of samsara, the impermanence of death, the precious human body, and karmic fruits and results.

That is why there is a saying in the four lines of Sakya Pandita: "If you are attached to yourself, you are not a bodhisattva. If you are attached to your life, you are not a good practitioner." There are two ways to be a consistent practitioner. One is to be dependent on outside time and inside emotions. Sometimes you will have time to do your practice, and even if you have negative emotions, you'll still practice. But as time gets squashed from outside, you will begin to lose your practice. And as emotions change from negative to positive, you'll begin to lose your practice. I'm not talking about everybody, but some people's practice is dependent on outside time and inside emotions, and when the situation changes, their practice falls apart. That is what makes people inconsistent with their practice, and it proves that they haven't thought through the four thoughts and the four noble truths well, because if they had, their practice wouldn't be dependent on outside time and inside emotions.

The other way to develop a consistent practice is to practice constantly throughout your lifetime, which will definitely cause you to progress throughout your life. But we still need guidance at each and every step of the path to make our practice flourish. If you contemplate the four thoughts and the four noble truths well, nothing becomes more important than the practice. Everything else in life has to be maintained, and you need to maintain it, but the most important thing to maintain is consistency in your practice. If you practice consistently and think about the four thoughts and the four noble truths, they will sting in your heart, but it's pleasure, not suffering, because they provide support for your practice to develop.

So, the yogi approached Dabyang and said, "Kyé, my dear friend Golden Bee, Dabyang. Why are you singing sad songs alone in the mountains? It seems the unexpected devil of death has taken a rope, tied up your dear karmic friend, and taken her away. Please don't be so sad. Plant a piece of bone in your heart." This is a Tibetan condolence, an expression that means "have strength in your heart."

The yogi says, "The practice of worldly Dharma is a good base for the practice of absolute Dharma." This is sarcasm. He continues, "The practice of Dharma is also for happiness." He means that although Dabyang is not happy, he has everything else that could make him happy and peaceful. Patrul Rinpoche is being sarcastic again. The "practice of worldly Dharma" means staying with your family, accumulating merit, and having a sense of what is virtuous and nonvirtuous, while trying to go more in the direction of what is virtuous. That kind of understanding is a very good base for absolute Dharma. "Worldly Dharma" is experiencing the pleasures of the five perceptions. In this case, he is saying that whatever you have, whatever you are surrounded with, you are well off, even though your friend is missing now.

He asks, "What is the use of absolute practice without results of happiness?" and continues by saying, "The practice of Dharma is also for happiness. What is the use of going for Dharma and renouncing happiness?" He is saying that ultimately enlightenment is happiness, and any practice of Dharma is for that result. Since Dabyang already had happiness in his life, why does he want to renounce life to practice Dharma? The yogi is testing him by asking him this. He tells him that although one friend has died, another friend can be found to put in her place. If Dabyang's renunciation were temporary and superficial, he'd say, "Yes, you're right. I'm not doing so badly."

The yogi is saying that even though Dabyang is very sad now, sadness and happiness are the nature of samsara. It's really no big deal. Even though he's sad now, he can experience a hundred times more happiness, so he shouldn't get all caught up in sadness. If Dabyang's renunciation were superficial, he'd say, "That's right. I don't really have to get all caught up in this emotion or make such a big deal out of it. I can continue to lead my life just fine." If he had said that, it would have shown that whatever his renunciation was, it didn't have deep meaning, and it wouldn't grow in his lifetime. The yogi is checking to see whether Dabyang has that kind of renunciation.

"Certain renunciations can be the evil influences of the demon, Radza." *Radza* means "king," and there's a story behind this. The story is that Guru Padmasambhava, after having finished building Samye Monastery, wanted to find someone to protect the monastery, so he sent one of Trisong Detsen's sons to rob an old burned down monastery. Nobody was living there, but no one could touch anything at that monastery because there was a devil or demonic being living there. If anybody tried to do anything there, they'd suddenly die. This demon was a very powerful being.

One day Guru Padmasambhava was in meditation in a cave, and early one morning this demonic Radza came and threw a stone as big as a yak on Guru Padmasambhava's head. Just then,

Guru Padmasambhava did the hook mantra and caught the demonic being right in front of him. Radza had many servants and monks in front of him, many monks on his left, and many laypeople on his right, with a lot of demons at his back. Guru Padmasambhava said, "Who are you?" and Radza said, "I am Bakar," which is a place, so he is the King of Bakar, and that is the monastery. At that point Guru Padmasambhava took Radza's heart and all the demons' hearts, and made them promise to protect Samye and all the people who do practice in Tibet. Then he gave some teachings to him, and Radza became a peaceful person. But he still had many people around him who were demonic and continued to harm beings even though Radza himself didn't. Often this guy tricks people by making them feel renunciation, and then he makes them move all their property to see how they'll react. So, if the renunciation is not coming from one's clear mind—if it's just some kind of circumstantial renunciation—it could be caused by Radza.

Pema Jyipa continues by asking, "Don't you know that this type of renunciation has no substance?" This is like when you meet your guru, and all of a sudden you feel very devoted, all your hair stands up on your body, tears run down your face, and your body starts to shake, but then two days later, you get disappointed in that lama or in yourself because you can't keep that feeling. Such devotion is good, but if you make a big deal out of it and hold onto it too much as a profound experience, that is wavering devotion that will turn this way and that. If you are dependent on that kind of feeling, you won't be a steady student or follow your teacher's teachings. You'll just go with the feelings of your own temporary, wavering mind, and then drop out.

"Sudden feelings of generosity and strong detachment are like the hala asu tree, which bears fruit only once, and then no more." Having that kind of renunciation and devotion, one might suddenly be very generous and start to give everything away, but when the devotion turns around, there's no more generosity. That generosity is like the hala asu tree that gives fruit only once, so it's not very meaningful in terms of a steady spiritual path.

"Renunciation can be like lightning in the sky, which flashes but a moment and vanishes without effect." That kind of renunciation, that kind of generosity, could be like lightning flashing just for a moment but not changing the sky. The point is that when we experience that kind of renunciation, we shouldn't take it too seriously, because if we do, we get off-balance in our life. The yogi points out these things to Dabyang, so he can reflect on what kind of renunciation and devotion he has, and on what his motivation for the path of enlightenment is. This will allow him to have some steadiness in his practice instead of temporarily flipping back and forth.

"The practice of worldly phenomena and Dharma is the true practice of intelligence. Don't you know such an attitude leads to the path of liberation?" This is sarcasm for some people, but not for everybody. If Dabyang's renunciation isn't really profound or if his understanding of Dharma isn't very good, when he hears something like that, he'll go for that kind of path, which would show that he is still attached to worldly things, and his renunciation is not complete.

"Taking pleasures as the path of enlightenment is the significance of the tantric path." True tantric practitioners use the pleasures of the five perceptions as the path of enlightenment. But even though these practitioners are engaged with the pleasures of the five perceptions, they are detached and, more and more, turn the perceptions and objects into the field of wisdom. If you merely try to imitate that, you know what you're going to get. Pema Jyipa says this to Dabyang at this stage to see whether his renunciation is profound. If it weren't, he would have thought, "Oh, this is it! Maybe I should try this."

"Remaining as king is the activity of the bodhisattva. Don't you know its benefits?" When a bodhisattva is on the tenth bhumi, they are born as a king or among the higher caste, so they can have more influence over people and turn people's minds toward the Dharma. Outside, they remain like a king but inside as a bodhisattva, and their action can be very profound and benefit a lot of people. So here, Pema Jyipa is telling Dabyang to just remain where he is, to just be who he is, and he will help many beings. He is testing him by comforting him to see if he buys that or not. If he had bought into that comfort, it would have proven that his renunciation was just temporary.

"If one is able to accumulate wealth, one can practice generosity. Don't you know this practice contains the six prajnaparamitas?" According to the prajnaparamita texts, Pema Jyipa is telling Dabyang that he doesn't have to renounce his wealth, but that only by holding onto his wealth can he be generous to people, and that contains the wisdom of the six prajnaparamitas. Also, this is a high-level practice for true bodhisattvas in order to accumulate so much merit. That's why they accumulate merit, which in turn accumulates even more merit for practicing the six prajnaparamitas. But here again, the yogi is testing him by consoling him in this way, giving him some hope at his own level. If he takes that advice, it is a direct expression of his incomplete renunciation and motivation.

"Without being completely convinced of what one promises to do, many conflicts and doubts arise in the mind, and one will not end up accomplishing what one sets out to do." If you are not convinced of what you're doing, and you do something with a lot of doubts and conflicts in your mind, you're not going to be able to accomplish that particular thing—or any other thing. Without the strength to face the difficulties of practice, you'll end up turning your face away from the Dharma. With temporary renunciation and temporary motivation, if you go to a difficult place to practice meditation, a place where there is no good shelter, food, or water, you'll stay there as long as those wavering emotions sustain you, but when those emotions are gone, you may stay there a little while longer because you're ashamed to come out, but then you will come out without much result. Then you'll start talking about the problems in your retreat, and how it just wasn't worth it, or you'll come out bragging about the retreat, and all the difficulties you faced, and what courage you had to finish it. That shows that you are turning away from the Dharma. If you don't go into retreat with complete renunciation, with complete understanding of the Dharma, you will come out with a negative concept of the retreat, as well as the Dharma, or you will come out with very strong pride. This is turning away from the Dharma.

"Without a complete understanding of renunciation, one will desire worldly life again but find that one has nothing left to turn to." Some people get into a mood where they give up everything, and they go into retreat, but when it doesn't work out the way they fantasized, they want everything back— their family, their nice homes, their furniture, their good job, their nice car—but since they renounced it all already, there is nothing left to come back to. That kind of renunciation is dangerous. If renunciation is complete, you carry on with the path until you complete the Dharma in an inner way. If renunciation is temporary, you go with the path and come back to the place where you started—with nothing. This happens a lot with people who are suffering from spiritual materialism.

"If one remains in a remote place without any realization, one will become bored, and one's practice will become dull; this person will be unable to continue." If you remain in a remote place without much realization or knowledge of the teachings or how to attain realization, you will sit there struggling and struggling, and life will become very boring. In the beginning, life will be somewhat challenging because of the struggle, but when the struggle is over, because you don't have realization, the practice will become more and more dull, and you won't be able to continue there.

"If one goes to the graveyard to practice chöd without having a good view, one will be influenced by the demons and become a servant of the devil." In Tibet, there's a tendency for some people to become bums. They don't really have a good excuse to be a bum, yet they accept themselves as bums and find that life to be very nice. These are good bums. But there are other people who are more than that, who have a good excuse to be a bum because they are chödpas and practice chöd. They travel all over the world to practice chöd. A genuine chöd practitioner will go to graveyards and practice chöd in places where there are a lot of fears or negative forces. They will, as they say, "perfect the quality of the place," and that makes their realization more profound. But those bums who use some big excuse about being chödpas, if they try to imitate that, they'll be influenced by the devil.

"If one merely acts like a siddha without possessing the qualities, one creates the circumstances for being reborn in Narak." That is, if one acts like a siddha without possessing the qualities, that person will turn into a hell being.

"If one changes one's circumstances without changing one's mind, one becomes the subject of others' laughter." If you change your mind—one day you're a Hindu, another day a Buddhist, another day a Zen practitioner, and so on—and you don't really perfect the qualities of the practice within your heart, people will laugh at you. It's the same with changing jobs, or changing your life in general. Whoever is like that becomes the subject of people's laughter.

"If one fails to contemplate before making an important commitment, one will get caught in the cycle of regressing." If you're not able to be steady and consistent with your actions and projects, others won't take you seriously. Telling others how clairvoyant you are without having the realization of emptiness distorts yourself and others. If you don't have a realization of emptiness, it is impossible to see the past and future. Some people can see thoughts very clearly, but if you tell everybody how clear your thoughts are, you're going to be in big trouble, and you'll lead others into big trouble, too. But if you hold the realization of emptiness and see how past, present, and future exist interdependently, without really existing, that kind of clarity is good.

"Trying to benefit others without perfecting compassion creates attachment." If you try to benefit others without really perfecting compassion, ultimately you will get caught up in attachment or aversion. If you try to be of benefit before you have complete realization, it's a very heavy thing. Regular benefit is okay, but in terms of spiritual help, it's not. So, you need to check clearly what comes into your mind before you try to benefit others.

A fundamental aspect of this text is to watch out for spiritual materialism and to watch out for a temporary, wavering mind. These days there are a lot of teachers who seem to be very profound, and some could be highly realized people—who knows? Like the Buddha said, don't speak for others. But those who are teaching new age things and taking bits of philosophy from all the religions might have temporary, wavering devotion, or temporary feelings of spiritual realization, but they are just trying to create a career or to make their life feel meaningful.

Part Six
When the yogi sang the song, Dabyang, the golden bee, felt uneasy, and he replied:

É MA! How wonderful!
In the thick of the remote forest,
the honest, peace-filled, happy yogi, Pema Jyipa,
willingly shares his concern with me, Golden Bee.
Surely, this is the sign of a reliable friend.
I, Dabyang, the sorrowful singer,
am the lucky recipient of your secret.
I, Dabyang, the miserable and lonely,
have the great fortune to receive your kind condolences.

It is wonderful to know that the two paths
(the path of worldly pleasures and the path of Dharma)
coexist and have great meaning.
I have stayed with the great lama and imagined doing nothing
but sitting practice, but this imagery was nothing
but a flash of excitement.

I have romanticized spending the rest of my life in the forest,
following the examples of the great yogis, but these fantasies
were filled with childish melodrama.

I have tried to befriend my enemies and lessen my
attachment to my relatives, but l failed to abolish bias.
I have given my heart and trust to the Three Jewels
and put the image of my guru on my head,
but I wasn't able to see my lama as inseparable from them.
Though I haven't boasted to others but praised them,
my humbleness was a mask of vanity.

However, through my karmic friend Ngakyen's death,
I have come to understand impermanence,
and my renunciation stems from this understanding.
I have written a promise in my heart.
In carrying the practice, I will whip myself with diligence.

My warm-hearted friend, Pema Jyipa, you have met a lama
who is inseparable from the Buddha himself, and with him
you have received many teachings and various texts.
Have you mastered the meanings of the words?
You have stayed in remote places;
have you true, natural realization?
You have sung many songs in rocky mountains;
have you results from your practice?
You have practiced nonattachment;
have you found equanimity?
You have watched the drama of samsara;
have you deepened your renunciation?

Sing me a song of true practice!
Sing me a song of the practical path!
Show me examples that will help me to understand the
nature of impermanence!
Tell me more of samsara!

Teach me the qualities of liberation.
Reveal the benefits of living in remote places.

I, Golden Bee, Dabyang, want to stay in remote mountains
with practice as my companion.
I want to see the drama of my mind.
I want to discuss this matter of realization with you.
This is what I want from my heart.

Commentary on Part Six

When the yogi sang these songs, Dabyang's mind felt uneasy,
and he asked Pema Jyipa to willingly share his concerns with
him. "Surely, this is the sign of a reliable friend." He continues
by saying, "It is wonderful to know that the two paths (the
path of worldly pleasures and the path of Dharma) coexist and
have great meaning." Dabyang is being a little sarcastic to the
yogi who'd told him that the experience of the six pleasures is
the essence of the tantric path and bestows great liberation.
Dabyang says he's glad to hear that, but he knows it isn't really
practical for him.

"I have stayed with the great lama and imagined doing
nothing but sitting practice, but this imagery was nothing but a
flash of excitement," Dabyang says. The yogi had told Dabyang
there were two different kinds of renunciation, one temporary
and the other really deep, and that a lot of people get lost in their
fantasies. So, Dabyang accepts the fact that his renunciation
was of the latter kind. Dabyang states that he has "romanticized
spending the rest of my life in the forest, following the examples
of the great yogis, but these fantasies were filled with childish
melodrama." Dabyang continues by saying, "I have tried to
befriend my enemies and lessen my attachment to my relatives,
but I failed to abolish bias." To really do that, you have to work
on developing a deeper realization.

In saying, "I have given my heart and trust to the Three
Jewels and put the image of my guru on my head, but I wasn't
able to see my lama as inseparable from them," Dabyang, by

194

just being a Tibetan, reveals his great, blind faith in the Three Jewels. He had given his heart and trust to the Three Jewels, always thinking they will protect him. He received teachings from his guru, ngöndro teachings and the guru yoga practice, in which he visualized the guru on top of his head, but he didn't completely give his heart and trust to the guru, and he didn't really see the guru as inseparable from the Three Jewels. If you don't see the guru as inseparable from the Three Jewels, the Three Jewels are just a fantasy in your mind and essentially can't touch your practice.

In the beginning of all Vajrayana teachings, the teacher tells you that your guru contains in an outer way the Buddha, Dharma, and Sangha, and in an inner way the guru, deity, and dakini, and secretly the dharmakaya, sambhogakaya, and nirmanakaya. So you don't need to look for another refuge object outside of your guru. But, of course, the guru has to be someone really good. That is why the Vajrayana teachings always explain that you should check out the qualities of the guru before you receive teachings, and that the guru also should check out the qualities of the students.

> My warm-hearted friend, Pema Jyipa, you have met a lama who is inseparable from the Buddha himself, and with him you have received many teachings and various texts. . . .
> Have you true, natural realization?

If you practice seriously, you'll have a very strong urge to talk and write and sing about your realization, and to share that with others to benefit beings. But if you follow those urges, it's nothing but desire. In the beginning of your practice in the mountains, if you felt the need to sing songs and express your feelings about the practice, you knew that you'd better not do it because you might be carried away by your emotions. But later on, when your practice becomes more stable and you have complete control over your emotions, then if you sing songs as you walk around in the mountains, those songs could be a way of arousing your devotion to your teacher in appreciation for your practice. It could also increase your awareness somewhat. So, that's good.

A lot of teachers sing songs when they pass that stage. They usually sing where there aren't any people, like in rocky mountains. There's something about singing in rocky mountains that deepens realization, but they don't sing before they get past that urge. Even if they have an urge, it's not because they feel proud of themselves, though it may sound like it. For example, Milarepa's songs may sound like they come from some sense of pride. But it's not pride as we know it, which holds on to ego. It is more or less from having mastered the paths and appreciating what he's mastered. These songs arise from realization. This may be the result of considerable effort, but because realization does not rely on emotional states or concepts, it is not made up; it's natural.

Realizing means "having a breakthrough in your ordinary emotions." I would say realization is seeing that mind is not substantial and tangible; it is empty of any forms and completely free of any texture. The word for "realization" is *lhakthong*, or *vipashyana*. *Thong* means "seeing." What you have not seen before, you're seeing now—an experience of mental continuum being changed into a new kind of experience. According to the Buddhist point of view, enlightenment is complete awareness, without any faults. Realization is what is realizing the faults, and then diminishing the faults through practice.

There can be many different realizations. For instance, it is easier to realize that all existent phenomena are impermanent in a gross way. It is harder to realize subtle impermanence— phenomena always changing, moment to moment—but both are a realization of the nature of existence. Another example is realizing that all existent phenomena have some sense of suffering and have the suffering of distortion. This is also a realization of the nature of phenomena. Also, there is the realization that all existent phenomena are empty in nature. Nothing inherently exists; everything is interdependently existent. The weather, the cosmos, the self, the ego—all are empty. Ego is just a reflection or belief that there is a self, though one never sees or experiences clearly what it is. It is empty. These are examples of realization.

To realize these points in your own mind takes practice. At this time, it can seem to us that phenomena are permanent and solid, and that there is joy in samsara, and that the self is real. Our minds are usually just that way. But through the teachings, one can realize that one's perceptions are false and see what is true. And when one has a breakthrough to this new kind of understanding of clarity, that's what's called realization, or true understanding. Realization does not have to be absolute. It could be just an intellectual realization. The quality of intellectual understanding has to come through practice. Otherwise, one will have a realization of selflessness that is not selflessness if one has not done practice. That would be just relative realization. It has to come through practice.

"You have practiced nonattachment; have you found equanimity?" This is a very important question to reflect on if you are really practicing mahamudra, or ati yoga, which is very common in this world right now. Many people seem to be practicing mahamudra and ati yoga. Or, if you're practicing any real path of Buddhism, you must have an attitude of equanimity as you go about your life. This is in the sense that you don't become attached when you have a good life, nor do you become disgusted or down when you face a bad life. There is a saying, "If one has an attitude of equanimity when bad circumstances come, it shows what a good practitioner is." Practitioners can seem so good and perfect, but when bad times come, they could be completely miserable. Therefore, you can only know a good practitioner by how well that person faces bad circumstances. If they have an attitude of equanimity, that shows some realization, some deep practice, and that their practice is reliable.

"You have watched the drama of samsara; have you deepened your renunciation?" This is very important to ask oneself because there are many questionable attitudes and much high-sounding talk going on right now—about "dancing in the world" and "staying like a lotus in the puddle of the world," or "walking the bodhisattva path, unattached to everything"—but there is nothing practical in that kind of talk, no realization. Of course, the bodhisattvas who are realized do live in the world like a lotus above the lake because they are realized, and they have an attitude of equanimity. Bad circumstances don't affect them at all. But they have very strongly renounced samsara. They have a strong inspiration to be liberated in their life and can't stand it when others suffer. So, they always have renunciation.

> Sing me a song of true practice!
> Sing me a song of the practical path!
> Show me examples that will help me
> to understand the nature of impermanence!
> Tell me more of samsara!

If you have really learned the four thoughts well—the precious human body, impermanence and death, karma, and suffering of samsara—and you contemplate them consistently in your daily practice, there is no way that your practice won't be good. If you haven't really contemplated the four thoughts at all, and you're practicing a very high meditation, your practice is only for temporary pleasure, or for a moment's entertainment. So, it's very important to think about the four thoughts because they're practical, true, and essential for living. Therefore, the four thoughts are described many times in the teachings. Many people get bored because they hear about it so many times, and it kind of depresses them, so they don't want to hear any more. They'd rather take some kind of tranquilizer to give them a little buzz. But teachers say the four thoughts are very important because if you have thoroughly contemplated them, your practice and your life will automatically turn toward the true Dharma.

"Teach me the qualities of liberation." This is very important. If you don't know what liberation is or what meditation is for, practice and liberation have no meaning. But if you contemplate the four thoughts, especially the suffering of samsara, then you'll develop renunciation, and you will have the inspiration to practice a really good, true path.

"I, Golden Bee, Dabyang, want to stay in remote mountains with practice as my companion." If you take the practice as your companion, then each and every moment that you are with your mind, you're also with your practice. If you have even a little bit of mindfulness, then practice becomes your companion during every moment of your life. But if you lose that mindfulness, if you lose the relationship with your practice, then it never becomes your companion. Staying in a remote place helps you develop mindfulness because there are fewer things to do. There's also a sense of loneliness, which makes the mindfulness quite clear, and practice becomes your companion. If practice is your companion, even though you experience the most miserable tragedy, since you know that's how things are anyway, you won't have feelings of guilt and fear and self-pity. Instead, you'll face the difficulties and cut through the tragedies, and accept them as relative phenomena, which more or less touches the part of them that is absolute and inscrutable and indescribable. Nothing can destroy that. Therefore, it is unchangeable, inscrutable. That is why it is called vajra practice, the Vajrayana.

"I want to see the drama of my mind." Most of us enjoy going to see dramas outside, and if it's something really true and practical, we enjoy it and say, "Oh, that's very good art." If you could have the same attitude toward your mind, without any attachment or aversion, you would really enjoy that, too. People enjoy watching nature shows—about animals and geology. In a relative sense, since they're about nature, you wouldn't say, "It should be like this! It shouldn't be like that." Instead, you just accept that it's nature and enjoy the show. On the other hand, even though your life is natural, often you don't enjoy your life that way at all. You have a lot of thoughts about how your life should or shouldn't be. But if you could have the same attitude about your life and every single phenomenon, you could really enjoy everything—the ocean, the park, people, even negative things and your own emotional conflicts. Every single phenomenon is naturally created in its own way. Everything is natural. There's nothing in the universe that isn't natural. Even unnatural things are natural, because without nature, they couldn't function in the world. If something functions, even though it was made, it's natural, because the act of making itself is natural. *Natural* doesn't really mean "that which isn't made." And there are some things that you can't make because they aren't natural.

In that sense, every single thing in the universe is natural and has its own field to function in, whether it is human-made or not. Therefore, you can enjoy everything as nature and have less of the mind that continually says, "It *should* be like this; it *shouldn't* be like that." Then your life will follow very simply. Even your body can be very entertaining. But it's hard not to have those "should and shouldn't" thoughts, especially when they have something to do with you. Therefore, you need to apply the practice, and it will give you the solution for how to experience thoughts and emotions but not be ruled by them. You must practice consistently; there is no point in practicing for a short time and then leaving. If you practice consistently in everyday life, with a strong idea of the four thoughts, you will develop a very open wisdom eye. That wisdom eye will lead your heart to true practice, so you will be able to free yourself from your ignorance and dominating concepts. We have that choice in this lifetime, but don't expect to have the choice in another lifetime, because you never know. It's not worth the risk. You could get lucky, but your chances are one in a million.

Part Seven
As Golden Bee, Dabyang, finished the song, the yogi Pema Jyipa thought to himself:

As I suspected, Golden Bee is generally a good and reliable being, steady in whatever he does.
It doesn't seem as if his motivation is inspired by excitement.

For the moment, at least, he seems to have
a deepened faith in the Dharma.
I should sing a song that is suitable for his mind.

Pema Jyipa thought a moment and then began to sing:

Kyé, kyé, my dear friend Golden Bee, Dabyang,
you have a saddened mind of renunciation,
and therefore make only short-term plans.
You have a desire to practice, which is a sign
that you have prayed much in your previous lifetimes.
You have understood all things that are compounded
are impermanent and like the play of magic.
You have renunciation and want
to leave the world of the eight worldly concepts.
You have the wish to stay in remote places, which is a sign
you have the karma to practice the teachings.
Your sharp mind understands the philosophy of karma:
what to abandon and what to accumulate.
You also know the activities of a true bodhisattva.
Finding the door of this path
indicates that you are blessed by a great noble being.

You fortunate little bee, I, the disciple of a great lama,
will sharpen your understanding
through the confidence I have from my experience.
You should listen open-heartedly to what I say.

Down there in the valley of samsara,
the beings are grasping at the magical play of phenomena.
Believing it is solid and static, they become deluded.
They grab continuously at their negative desires,
which creates suffering that burns like a great forest fire.
They've turned their backs on virtues so many times,
happiness has become as rare for them
as encountering a star in the daytime.

Everyone is getting involved in so many negative deeds,
it is as if the Dark Ages were about to drop upon them
the moment the sun has set.
These beings are like grains in a mill
being sucked down into the lower realms of existence.
As there is increasingly less pleasure in the human realm,
there is an increase of suffering in the lower realms,
as karma works in great detail.

In ancient times, people could fly great distances
with natural powers.
Their riches could compete with those in heaven.
Such leaders as Khorlo Gyur Gyal (King of the
Turning Wheel) ruled the lands.
He turned fields into gold.
He was king of the four continents.
There was the law of the ten virtues,
and one could visit the heaven realms after death.
So many were born in heaven,
where people are naturally virtuous.
As all were born from flowers in heaven,
the fields were full of blossoms.

In this Dark Age, the natural environment
has been conquered by concrete and steel.
The ploughed fields fill the air with dust.
Wealth is measured in blood and meat.
The leaders are like butlers for hell.
One of the properties of their function is creating
war and killing.
Their dependents are unfortunate beings.
Their laws are deceitful and designed to benefit only themselves.
The more power they have, the more they lie.
They go on tours to the lower realms.
In the hottest hell realm, the population is increasing.
In battle the demons win. Disease flourishes.

The king on the throne uses trickery.
Without good reason, he punishes his subjects.
He deceitfully finds faults in innocent people.
With his sneaky mind, he destroys others, along with himself.

The lamas under their umbrellas use trickery.
They use Dharma for their own means.
They make clever assumptions in the pretense
of clairvoyance.
They sell empowerments.
With little power, they recite mantras
to protect the powerful and keep peace with them.
With no inner practice, they spend their time
performing rituals rather than sitting.

Mountain retreatants are also sneaky.
They sleep like corpses in their retreat huts, but when
sensing someone approaching, they quickly sit erect.
Before their sponsors pay a visit,
they hide all their belongings, and then exclaim to them:
"Oh, I don't have this; I don't have that!"

Most ordinary people are tricky.
Their minds are like a potter's wheel.
Checking carefully, they know just how to turn the wheel
in order to manipulate the clay.
Their words are like the hands of a blacksmith.
A little bang here, a little bang there,
and the metal is just the right shape!
Whatever gets them what they want.
Their promises are like dramatic summer weather:
one minute blue, the next black.
Their relationships are like a fly's tongue:
sticking out only when there's food to be had.
Their appreciation is like a painting:
there's a picture in the front, but the back is blank.

Their devotion is like a dish of *lung*:
it dissolves once it touches the tongue.

Students are tricky, too. Their studies are uneven,
like a tadpole's body. At the beginning,
their enthusiasm for learning swells their head,
but sooner or later it dwindles down.
Their practice is like a frog's mouth:
only there when it's time to listen
and gone when it's time to practice.

When lying gurus with sneaky minds
try to turn their Dharma-less behavior into Dharma,
when they teach essence practices without any realization,
when this earth is filled with mischief,
who can lead an honest life?
When centuries are full of devious practitioners,
who can learn the pure philosophy?
When kings break their own laws, who can one trust?
When lamas are merely looking to benefit themselves,
who will benefit the vulnerable ones?
When leaders rob their own subjects' wealth,
who will protect them?

Kyé-ma, kyé-ma—
my mind is completely saddened.
Between the teeth of impermanence,
the sufferers of the three realms
run around grasping as if all were permanent,
spending their whole lives benefiting themselves.
At death, they beat their fists against their chest.

As one continually contemplates how to lead one's life tomorrow,
one pushes the benefits of Dharma away for the next life.
This morning's body may be called dead tonight. See how it is?
Tomorrow or the next life—who knows which will come first?

I, the little yogi, Pema Jyipa,
have met a guru who is the real Buddha,
who, with great kindness and compassion,
has accepted me as his disciple.

My devotion and motivation are unwavering.
My faith has maintained its purity.
Whatever I asked my teacher came spontaneously,
without fabrication.
My actions were natural and uncontrived.
My attitude was never tricky.
I was never a face-licker and back-biter.
My mind is entrusted to one person, who is my deity.
I've never searched for refuge in others.
I've stayed a long time with this noble being
and have studied various texts with other learned scholars.
Thus, I know the difference between the true Dharma
and that which merely seems like Dharma.

Golden Bee, Dabyang! If you have really found true renunciation,
you must abandon that which only appears to be Dharma
and find the true Dharma practice.
When one searches for the path of Dharma,
one experiences a feeling of grief that leads to renunciation.
Often this grief is not the true grief
that leads to the understanding of samsaric suffering
but is rather like a feeling of repulsion toward one's life.
This grief that may only seem to be leading to renunciation
is inspired by a heavy, pessimistic mind,
a sense of helplessness that is circumstantial and temporary—
the loss of a dear one, weariness of life,
or a temporary gathering of sad emotions.

Although it may seem like grief
leading to pure renunciation, it is not.

There are two types of renunciation.
One is motivated by pure understanding.
The other, which only seems to be motivated by pure understanding,
is often inspired by the excitement to change one's dress
into robes for show, as a spiritual sign;
the wish to leave worldly circumstances
in order to relax in a pleasant retreat place;
the desire to recite mantras for worldly gain;
the wish to go on pilgrimage in order to have a nice vacation;
or a hope to gain respect from the public.

Although it may seem like pure renunciation, it is not.

There are two types of practitioners in retreat.
One is very diligent.
The other, who only *seems* to be diligent,
is often very strict on the outside
but sloppy inside, casual and undisciplined,
interested in improving worldly skills in retreat,
and always trying to distract themselves from practice,
passing the time sleeping.

Although this person may appear to be in retreat,
there is no essence in it.

There are two types of practitioners with a disgust
for samsaric suffering.
One understands the true nature of samsara.
The other only seems to understand
but actually is not succeeding in the world
and only wants to escape.
Unable to cope with life, just wanting to be a madperson,
this practitioner engages in thoughtless action,
has nothing worldly to give up anyway,
has little intelligence and skill,
and therefore feels there's nothing better to do.

Although it may seem like true disgust for samsara, it is not.

There are two types of pilgrims.
One has pure motivation.
The other only seems to but actually
only has interest in seeing the world,
with little desire to visit holy places
and no devotion to them,
circumambulating without knowing the benefit,
and using pilgrimage as an excuse to beg while
carelessly and mindlessly running around.

Although one may seem like a true pilgrim,
this activity has no essence.

There are two types of retreat practice.
One, with a pure understanding of the practice, and the
other, which only *seems* to be genuine when one recites
mantras without doing the visualization, does completion
practices without having confidence in them,
desires power by reciting wrathful deity mantras,
counts one's accomplishments, and
practices only for gain in this life.

Although this may appear to be good retreat practice, it is not.

There are two types of refuge.
One is done with great sincerity.
The other only seems to be sincere but is focused on how
many recitations are left, reciting without trust and with
no understanding of the differences between each of the
refuge objects, reciting without knowing the significance
of each object of refuge, and
reciting for the sake of worldly happiness.

Although this may seem like pure refuge practice, it is not.

There are two types of bodhicitta mind.
One type is pure.
The other is inspired by
being goodhearted for one's own self-image, wishing for
fruition in the form of worldly luxuries, personal biases, and
favoring certain beings over others, and the tendency to
think one already has a bodhicitta mind without
understanding the advice given for the bodhisattva vow.

Although this may seem like pure bodhicitta mind, it is not.

There are two types of visualization practice.
One is motivated by deeper understanding.
The other is practiced without clear appearance but
with a proud concept of oneness with the deity,
with no understanding of deity-pride except for appearance,
with indulgence toward and grasping at
one's ordinary self as the deity,
without compassion in visualizing wrathful images, and
without understanding the purity, completeness,
and ripeness of one's visualization practice.

This may seem to be visualization practice,
but it's only the cause of samsara.

There are two types of inner practice.
One is practiced with great understanding.
The other only seems to be but is not, such as doing the
channels practices without understanding luminosity,
not understanding the magical qualities of phenomena
but practicing dream yoga,
doing practice with a consort without unknotting channels,
practicing mahamudra and maha ati without understanding
the self-liberation of one's delusions, and
getting caught up in grasping appearance in tögal practice.

Although these may seem like completion practices,
they have no essence.

There are two types of benefiting beings
after one has reached the fruition stage.
One is truly beneficial.
The other only seems beneficial but is not.
When one waits for clairvoyance to appear,
one is seduced by demons, one tries to create an image of
oneself as a teacher of Dharma, one tries to get disciples
without helping them gain realization, and
one teaches important texts without any experience.

Although this may seem beneficial, it is not.

These fifty-five points are not to be used to look at others' faults.
They are to be used as a mirror to see one's own.
These I use to see myself clearly.
You should also see them in this way.
If you practice to impress others, many obstacles will arise.
So, check carefully, again and again.

Be consistent. These words have little poetry,
but the meaning is rich.
These words have been passed down to me from my lama.
This is my advice.
If your heartfelt wish is to practice,
you should not make an issue of your practice,
but keep it to yourself.
You shouldn't put off your practice by making future plans.
It is important not to look for your practice outside of yourself.

True practice is like an appendage;
when you need it, it's right there.
At each and every moment of practice, you must have courage!
At each moment you must clarify the practice.

At each moment you must make sure your practice is immaculate.
Even if it's only daily practice, you must dedicate the merit.
Even if it's only every morning, you must have good motivation.
You must be sure every session is flawless.
Never forget your practice;
even while doing mundane activities,
remember your practice at all times.
If your practice is not refined,
then your "big practitioner image" will have no essence.

Being lazy in retreat, mindlessly leading your life
in an isolated place, and thinking indulgently
about the luxuries of living in a remote area
are the three most wasteful things.

Do you understand, Golden Bee?

1. Don't be happy when you're leisurely and comfortable,
    but be happy when you're suffering.
    Leisure and comfort are the sources of the five kleshas.
    Suffering is the source of karmic purification.
    Suffering is the gift of the lama.

2. Don't be happy when someone praises you,
    but be happy when someone disgraces you.
    Praise fertilizes the ego.
    Disgrace reveals your thoughts.
    Unfavorable words are god's grand gift.

3. Don't be happy when you're important.
    Importance puffs you up with pride and increases jealousy.
    Through humbleness, you become open and easy,
    and your practice flourishes.
    The low seat is the noble being's seat.

4. Don't be happy if you're wealthy,

but be happy if you're poor.
Wealth must be constantly protected.
If one is poor, through hardships
one uses the time to accomplish realization.
The transient lifestyle is the practitioner's lifestyle.

5. Don't be happy if someone is generous with you,
   but be happy if someone robs you.
   Generosity must be paid back.
   Theft exhausts one's negative karma of debt.
   Contentment is the general wealth of the noble beings.

6. Don't be happy with relatives,
   but be happy surrounded by enemies.
   Relatives are obstacles toward one's liberation.
   Enemies are the objects of the perfection of patience.

Equanimity is the point of practice.
If your heartfelt wish is to practice,
you should follow these six points.
If you truly want to wander, you should follow these.
The six points are the most important source of the practice.
These are the teachings passed down from my father lama.
This life is filled with happiness, as is the next. A la la!

É MA! Golden Bee, son of the goddess:
The place on the high flower mountain
is the pure realm of the Goddess, Tara.
It is the great bliss of Avalokiteshvara.
It is the place where Pema Jyipa practiced.
Look at the mountain, which itself is the shape
of the noble body of Avalokiteshvara's peaceful mind mudra.
Look at the rock, which is itself the speech of the noble being,
Avalokiteshvara's countless mantras,
appearing naturally on the mountain.
Look at the bursting green of the floating trees,

which are themselves the perfection
of Tara's turquoise pure land.
It is surrounded by poisonous snakes,
which no devil-minded being would dare cross.
In the foreground, the flowers have blossomed,
which are themselves the very manifestation
of Padmasambhava and have appeared to free beings.
At the bottom of the mountain is
the beautiful cave-palace of the noble mother, Tara.
It is the time for the noble mother to benefit beings.
In the heart of the mountain is the cave
of Pema Jyipa, the yogi, worshipper of Avalokiteshvara;
the reciter of the six-syllable mantra;
the practitioner of kindness and compassion;
the follower of the blissful path
of the bodhisattvas, sons and daughters of the buddhas.

Even desiring suffering, I experience only happiness.
I travel from one happy place to another. A la la!
Ultimate happiness, unchangeable:
I pray to the victorious guru whose blessing is
all-pervading. A la la!

I practice the deity Avalokiteshvara;
the nectar is not far away. A la la!
These "A la la's" are amazing miracles.
Do you understand, Son of the Goddess?
I, Pema Jyipa, conclude the points here. A la la!

Commentary on Part Seven
We all try to be bodhisattvas, and when we do small things
we think, "Oh this is great! Today I did something like a
bodhisattva." But you are a bodhisattva only if you don't ask for
anything in return, not even a smile. We all do bits of this and
that, which may seem like a bodhisattva's activity, and we hold
onto that very proudly. But when a person changes their mind

and shows some disapproval, we fall apart. From the beginning, that is not bodhisattva activity. So, don't have the mind that expects something in return; just do it. If you do something really good, you'll get the credit; nobody else will receive it. According to karma, you're the only one who'll receive that credit.

Pema Jyipa is being very humble and isn't really saying to Dabyang, "I will be your lama." He knows that Dabyang has met a lama before, so he tells him what a fortunate little bee he is to be a disciple of a great lama too, and that he'll sharpen his understanding through the confidence he's gained from his own experience. Pema Jyipa continues:

> Down there in the valley of samsara,
> the beings are grasping at the magical play of phenomena.
> Believing it is solid and static, they become deluded.
> They grab continuously at their negative desires,
> which creates suffering that burns like a great forest fire.

Because we see things as solid and substantial, we have a good excuse for our grasping mind. Because we grasp, our desires for negative things naturally increase, and this brings a lot of karma for us to suffer, like a burning forest fire.

"They've turned their backs on virtues so many times, happiness has become as rare for them as encountering a star in the daytime." We're caught in the desire of negative forces and lack the morality to do virtuous things, so we rarely have happiness in our lives; it's as rare as a star in the daytime sky. I definitely think that most of our present luxury must have come from previous lifetimes because our actions in this lifetime are so negative.

"Everyone is getting involved in so many negative deeds, it is as if the Dark Ages were about to drop upon them the moment the sun has set." In one way or another, everyone in our society is interested in money and business. Business is based on greed, and greed always produces negative actions. We're all involved in that. So, the age we are facing right now is like when the sun sets and darkness is about to fall. Face it or not, like it or not, that's the way it is. I think a lot of lamas try not to worry people about this, but I don't think that's quite fair. If something is true, people should know it. Maybe then people could help themselves a little bit, even if they can't help others.

"These beings are like grains in a mill being sucked down into the lower realms of existence." I can't really speak according to Patrul Rinpoche's experience, but I'm sure he could see what goes on in the lower realms and also what goes on here. He's saying that the population of beings in the lower realms was always huge in the beginning, but as time goes by, it's becoming even more populated down there, and happiness is also vanishing here. That's a sign that we're not very smart in terms of figuring out what is good for us, and we don't know the cause and effect of our karma. Pema Jyipa continues:

In ancient times, people could fly great distances
with natural powers.
Their riches could compete with those in heaven.
Such leaders as Khorlo Gyur Gyal (King of the
Turning Wheel) ruled the lands.

People in ancient times were naturally very moral, and because of this, they had many riches, so much so that their riches could compete with those in the heavens. Many times, even heaven beings were envious of beings in this realm. There were kings like Khorlo Gyur Gyal, who was a bodhisattva on the tenth bhumi who had a chance to become a buddha in this realm. When there is no cause and circumstance for a buddha to appear, then they appear as Khorlo Gyur Gyal. When they appear in this way, there are eight different riches around them that work for them, and at that time, people definitely had to obey the laws of the ten virtues.

In those olden days, through a great deal of merit, one might become a king with superior power. Such superior power included having a superior nature, along with a superior consort or queen, a minister, a horse, an elephant, a wish-fulfilling jewel, and a wheel. The wheel is described as something the king spins in the space in front of him to subjugate all his enemies. The horse could fly. The minister has a very intelligent mind, and his wife is beautiful and pleasant. The elephant has eight heads and sixteen tusks, with a complete set of everything. The horse is for travel and the elephant for war, and both come complete with luxurious fabrics and adornments. The jewel fulfills wishes. It is rare for a person to have this form, and only the buddhas or bodhisattvas who are in or above the eighth bhumi have it. This is a "universal monarch."

For example, in the time of the Tibetan king Songsten Gampo, there was a very strict enforcement of the laws of the ten virtues. Hundreds and thousands of people were killed for not obeying those laws. But of those who were killed, many were his own manifestations whom he killed so that people would feel really strongly about the ten virtues and being reborn in the heaven realm after they died. Though it wasn't liberation, it was definitely a good result after leaving this realm. When you're born in heaven, you're born in a flower, not from a mother. Because there were so many people reborn in heaven, that accounted for the many flowers blooming there at that time.

> In this Dark Age, the natural environment
> has been conquered by concrete and steel.
> The ploughed fields fill the air with dust.
> Wealth is measured in blood and meat.

In this dark age of iron, our natural environment is being "conquered by concrete and steel" with buildings everywhere. There are so many companies building everywhere. Not that long ago, it was enough for one family to have one shelter, and they were very happy living there. Nowadays, we're so sophisticated and have so many ways and excuses to become depressed. We have emotional conflicts with each other, so each individual needs an individual shelter; each family member must have a separate room. Not only that, we often think we need an entirely separate house. In the past, farmers planted their fields once a year. I'm sure that a long, long time ago they didn't even have to plant. But later, they only planted once a year and were happy with the crops they had. But as humans become more and more greedy, they plant nonstop, so dust is always blowing.

If you examine what wealth basically is, our digestive wealth mainly consists of meat and blood. People spend hundreds and thousands of dollars on meat. Food is a necessity, and most of our money goes to buy meat. I know a lot of Tibetan lamas who say, "Eat meat. It's very good for your health, and to practice Dharma, you need to have good health, so you should eat meat." That could be true, but only if you're a really serious practitioner. Otherwise, if you're just hanging around, that is not wise advice.

Patrul Rinpoche never advises anyone to eat meat. His students were strict vegetarians, but occasionally he ate meat. In fact, once Patrul Rinpoche was in his retreat center in Tibet when some people put up tents on the other side of the mountain where there was a lot of grass and many animals were grazing. When Patrul Rinpoche's students saw that, they became very excited and told him. Patrul Rinpoche said, "Oh, we should go down there and check out who is there." So, all the students went there with Patrul Rinpoche, who prostrated to that place from a mile away. There was a very tall, tough-looking guy with his long hair tied up and wearing guns, and the other scoundrels around him looked just like him. When this guy saw Patrul Rinpoche, he said, "Old dog, welcome! Come, come. Come and eat."

All his students were offended when they heard him call Patrul Rinpoche an old dog, but Patrul Rinpoche seemed to be paying a lot of respect to this guy, so they kept quiet. Then the man said, "Bring the lunch." A big plate of meat was handed around to all the disciples, and to Patrul Rinpoche, too. That day Patrul Rinpoche ate meat like he'd never seen it before. He ate everything he was given. His students were very uptight when they were given meat and couldn't believe their eyes when Patrul Rinpoche ate it. But then the students ate all their meat, and they left.

When they got back, someone asked Patrul Rinpoche, "Is it true that from now on we can eat meat?" Patrul Rinpoche got very angry and said, "No way!" Then someone said, "You just ate meat. What do you mean 'no way'?" He replied, "That's different. All the animals that were killed there are definitely liberated now. This is not an ordinary case but an extraordinary one."

"The leaders are like butlers for hell." Of course, butlers walk with you from an entrance to meet "the big shot." So, the leaders of this dark generation are more or less like butlers for hell because they lead you into entering so many different kinds of negative situations.

"Their laws are deceitful and designed to benefit only themselves." It's true that there are laws that protect people until they're proven guilty, but people take advantage of that. Lawyers sometimes take advantage and make a lot of money from tricking people and manipulating the law in this and that way. Though many laws seem to be very profound in theory, in practice they can seem like they were written by people who are merely trying to benefit themselves. Otherwise, why would there be a need for so many lawyers?

> The more power they have, the more they lie.
> They go on tours to the lower realms.
> In the hottest hell realm, the population is increasing.
> In battle the demons win. Disease flourishes.

Before Tibet was invaded by the Chinese, there were stories about some Tibetans who could see beings in other realms. They could see special protectors were engaged in war, and when they lost, they ran away to India. There were even a lot of sounds coming from this realm, like bumping and things like that, although you couldn't see anything. There was a time when the Dharma protectors were in a weak spot. I'm sure the wisdom-eye Dharma protectors were beyond that kind of control, but others definitely lost.

"The lamas under their umbrellas use trickery." In Tibet, lamas sometimes travel with someone holding an umbrella over them. I think the practice originated in ancient China.

Some of them use Dharma for their own means.
They make clever assumptions in the pretense of clairvoyance.
They sell empowerments.
With little power, they recite mantras
to protect the powerful and keep peace with them.

Year after year, lamas perform rituals in the homes of important people to remove their obstacles for the coming year and to keep faith with powerful leaders and important sponsors. "With no inner practice, they spend their time performing rituals rather than sitting." Because these lamas' job is to perform rituals here and there, they don't really spend much time practicing the teachings and working on their realization. Not all lamas are like this, but some are, so that's the point being made here.

Students are tricky too. Their studies are uneven,
like a tadpole's body. At the beginning,
their enthusiasm for learning swells their head,
but sooner or later it dwindles down.

In the beginning, Dharma students make a big effort, but as time goes on, their efforts often diminish.

When lying gurus with sneaky minds
try to turn their dharmaless behavior into Dharma,
when they teach essence practices without any realization,

when this earth is filled with mischief,
who can lead an honest life?

When these types of things are going on, it's very hard to
lead an honest life. There is a story about a king who heard it
was going to start raining in a few weeks and that whoever
drank that water would go crazy. So, the king covered his well,
and everyone else drank the rainwater and went crazy. The king
alone remained sane, but then his people perceived him as the
only one who had gone crazy, so eventually the king had to
drink the water, too.

My actions were natural and uncontrived.
My attitude was never tricky.
I was never a face-licker and back-biter.
My mind is entrusted to one person, who is my deity.

For the real tantric practitioner, the guru is the deity, and
the deity is the guru. There is no separation between the deity
and the guru. Marpa made a big mistake when he prostrated to
the deity instead of to Naropa, who was initiating him into the
deity's mandala.

I've never searched for refuge in others.
I've stayed a long time with this noble being
and have studied various texts with other learned scholars.

According to genuine Vajrayana practice, the guru himself
is the embodiment of refuge. No one is considered separate
from the guru. One must know the guru is the refuge object
and deepen that understanding more and more with the guru's
teachings. You have to stick with a teacher for a while because
if you don't, it's very hard to learn anything. A mother has to
teach her kids how to run, but first she has to teach them how
to crawl and then to walk. Once kids can run, they might fall
down, but because they were trained well, they get back up and

continue on their own. So, you have to be with your teacher to practice for a while to be able to know what you're supposed to do and how to overcome obstacles and the growing internal, emotional problems. When that's done, then you can depend on books and computers, but mainly on your practice.

Patrul Rinpoche studied with about a hundred and twenty different scholars and teachers. It's not true that you can't study with other teachers, but this is something that comes later. Of course, at first you stick with one teacher until you completely find your lineage. Then you can go around and receive other teachings, or if not that, you could receive some blessings. For instance, for a serious practitioner, just to get a few words of transmission from a serious teacher can be very, very powerful. Serious practitioners do that a lot, and it's something that can be very effective for your practice.

Knowing what merely seems like Dharma but is not Dharma might motivate you to have the true realization or true practice of Dharma. The fifty-five points are very poetically stated in Tibetan, and were passed down to Patrul Rinpoche (or Pema Jyipa) from his lamas, so now he passes them on to Dabyang. To pass something down could be compared to poking a hole into a yak's nose to tame or domesticate the animal. When the animal is really steady, you could give that animal to a child when they're old enough. We have a tradition of passing down knowledge in Tibetan Buddhism, especially in the Nyingma lineage. But it's more or less our responsibility as to how to live our lives, so teachers don't interfere as much. For example, you wouldn't go to the teacher to ask, "Should I do this, or should I do that?" You'd depend on your own strength and understanding to make those decisions.

For a certain length of time, it's very important for the teacher to lead you. But then when the teacher gives you the reins—like Patrul Rinpoche giving this advice—you should take them. For instance, Yeshe Dorje, Patrul Rinpoche's best friend who studied under the same teacher he did, wanted to become a layman when he was twenty-three. Everyone went a little crazy about this and told his teacher to advise him not to do that. But when Yeshe Dorje went to see his teacher, the teacher told him, "I have given you the leash. Now it's up to you what you want to do with it. You know best what you want to do." Beyond that, he didn't say another word.

So, "these fifty-five points are not for looking at other people's faults but to look at our own." If we can see our own faults, we will definitely know how to change them into their opposite because we're smart enough, and we know the Dharma well enough to know what is right. But since we can have a lot of pollution in our Dharma practice, these will point out that pollution.

If your heartfelt wish is to practice, you should not make an issue of practice, but keep it to yourself. If you make an issue out of how you're going to do this and that, it's as if you really want to get across the point that—since you're doing this and that—aren't you wonderful? Aren't you doing something good? That's egocentric. So, Patrul Rinpoche is saying not to do that. Keep the practice completely private. There is a saying, "There is no fault in the tantra. If you practice tantra, tantra brings fruition very quickly, but if you make an issue of it and talk about it, it loses its qualities."

"At each and every moment of practice, you must have courage!" You really must have courage in your practice because there are so many obstacles that you'll attempt to indulge in and that will prevent you from doing practice. So, have the courage to pass through all the obstacles and to do your practice. Courage is facing what you must face in each and every moment and doing the practice. If you indulge in circumstances and the things that come along as obstacles to your practice, even if you're very bold in general, you won't have courage in your practice, for sure.

"At each moment you must clarify the practice." There are sixty minutes in an hour, and in those sixty minutes, 3600 seconds. So, when we practice for an hour, we have to pass that many moments. Without those moments, there is no such thing as one hour. As you pass that many seconds and minutes, you must be able to recognize each thought that comes up in your mind. And when you guide your awareness this way, day after day, being mindful in each and every moment, that is the right direction. Whatever weaknesses there are in your practice, you will naturally draw closer and closer to the teachings. After a while, when you read a teaching, it won't remain as theory; it becomes experience.

Even in daily practice, you must dedicate the merit. To dedicate the merit, we may think we have to attend a big ceremony or do something very virtuous that we can really be proud of, but that's not always true. You should dedicate your merit after every session. If you practice for an hour each day, dedicate that. You shouldn't think, "Oh, I didn't do much today. It was just an hour; it's not a big deal. I don't see much merit in it, so why dedicate it? How does it really benefit to dedicate it?" You should dedicate it. As time goes by, and you learn more about it, you will see what the point of that is.

Never forget your practice. Even while doing mundane activities, remember your practice at all times. We have a saying in Tibetan, "Virtue is as we walk and sit, as we eat and drink." Even when you're involved in mundane things, your mouth is still free to recite some mantras, and your mind is free to be mindful. If you do these things completely and with good motivation, virtue *is* as you go and sit, eat and drink. When we eat and drink, we often don't know how involved we can be and sometimes overeat or drink too much. Animals have been killed for one good dish. Patrul Rinpoche is saying that even with your mundane life and activities, you must have a good mind and apply the practice in whatever you're doing.

Being lazy in retreat, mindlessly leading your life
in an isolated place, and thinking indulgently
about the luxuries of living in a remote area
are the three most wasteful things.

First, being lazy in retreat does not accomplish anything spiritually. "Mindlessly leading your life in an isolated place" without any reason is the second wasteful thing. The third thing is "thinking indulgently about the luxuries of living in a remote area." This is like saying, "Oh, I wish I could go to that mountain to stay. It would be so quiet and peaceful and relaxing." If you have concepts about going to a mountain for retreat for the sake of your enlightenment, then that is something valuable. But if you're just going there to indulge in the luxury of your physical body and quietness of your mind, it shows you're a coward, unable to face what you have to face.

1. Don't be happy when you're leisurely and comfortable, but be happy when you're suffering.
   Leisure and comfort are the sources of the five kleshas.
   Suffering is the source of karmic purification.
   Suffering is the gift of the lama.

If you have leisure, you'll feel the need to maintain that leisure, which causes you to get involved in desire, anger, jealousy, and ignorance, because to maintain that leisure, these negative qualities will naturally flare up. But if you're suffering, you'll recognize the nature of your mind more. Because you're desperate to help your mind, you'll become more desperate for meditation, in the same way that when you're sick, you're more desperate for medicine.

"Suffering is the source of karmic purification." Whatever you suffer is the fruit of your previous karma. Karma is not something like a solid wall, something completely separate from you that you can point out. Karma is what goes on in your mind. What goes on in your mind is dependent on your environment, and your environment is dependent on what you did in previous lives. So, what you did in previous lives provides your environment, and your environment provides your mind. That is the fruit of karma.

2. Don't be happy when someone praises you,
   but be happy when someone disgraces you.
   Praise fertilizes the ego.
   Disgrace reveals your thoughts.
   Unfavorable words are god's grand gift.

If someone praises you and tells you what nice hair you
have, what a beautiful face you have, what nice skin you have,
that is fuel for your ego, and psychologically it's not healthy for
you. But if someone disgraces you, there must be some truth to
their criticism for you to feel disgraced. If there isn't, then that
person is just crazy. But if they've made a point and you see
your fault, that disgrace becomes a mirror for your faults. Then
you're able to remedy that fault.

"Unfavorable words are god's grand gift." We're not talking
about "Almighty God" or anything like that. This is just a
colloquial term. If people are unfavorably gossiping about you,
that often proves you were serious about whatever it was you
were involved with.

3. Don't be happy when you're important.
   Importance puffs you up with pride and increases jealousy.
   Through humbleness, you become open and easy,
   and your practice flourishes.
   The low seat is the noble being's seat.

Don't be happy when you're high up the social ladder, but be happy when you're low. If someone puts you up high, I definitely think you'll develop some pride, and to maintain the pride, you'll be subject to a lot of jealousy toward those who are equal to or higher than you.

"Through humbleness, you become open and easy, and your practice flourishes." It's very obvious that it's a lot easier to talk to a bum than to talk to a president. Even if I had the opportunity to talk to the president, if it wasn't about something political, it might be very stilted. But if it were political, conversation with the president would be more open and natural. Remaining low keeps you humble, open, and easy going.

4. Don't be happy if you're wealthy,
   but be happy if you're poor.
   Wealth must be constantly protected.
   If one is poor, through hardships
   one uses the time to accomplish realization.
   The transient lifestyle is the practitioner's lifestyle.

This isn't an easy idea for Americans, but that's the view we must have in our mind, so we can better cope with life. If we have a static view that we must be happy and rich, then we aren't able to cope with the way circumstances really flow in our life. Having wealth requires that you constantly protect it, and not only must you have thoughts about how to protect it, you also have a lot of thoughts about how to increase it. Then, if it doesn't increase, you get depressed, and if you feel insecure about your wealth, you become fearful. So, if you're rich, you constantly live with depression and fear.

5. Don't be happy if someone is generous with you,
   but be happy if someone robs you.
   Generosity must be paid back.
   Theft exhausts one's negative karma of debt.
   Contentment is the general wealth of the noble beings.

If someone is generous with you, according to karma, you'll have to pay that generosity back somehow. There are two types of beings you can be generous to—venerable beings and victims. If someone is suffering or experiencing hunger, that is a victim. If you give something to a person like this, it's probably because you want to help them. But if you give an offering to someone who's venerable, you expect merit from your offering. Whenever you have a wish to receive some karma from an offering, that merit diminishes. It's best if you have no hope to receive anything in return. Regardless, both the victim and the venerable will have to pay you back. Someone who's really venerable pays you back with the power of their realization in your present lifetime, in your next lifetime, or in the bardo. But someone who just pretends to be venerable has to pay you back from their karmic debt, and that is very dangerous.

There is a story about a lama in Tibet named Lingje Repa, who was a great teacher. One day as he was teaching by a lake, he started saying, "Don't take money, don't take money." His students asked him why he was saying that, and he told them he saw someone there who was suffering tremendously. They asked, "Who? We don't see anything." He asked them if they wanted to see, and they told him yes. So, by his supernatural power and realization, he made the lake disappear, and there at the bottom of the lake was this gigantic fish covered with thousands and thousands of small animals who had made their home in his flesh, eating his flesh and blood. Lingje Repa told them that this fish had previously been a lama named Tsangla Tanakchen, who was very popular and renowned throughout Tibet. Everyone invited him places, and he said "PHET" here and there, and collected many offerings from people. But because he didn't actually have realization, he had to pay back those beings from his karmic debt. The point is, if you have realization, then you're able to help. If you don't, then you must pay back others' generosity from your karmic debt. There is no way around that.

6. Don't be happy with relatives,
   but be happy surrounded by enemies.
   Relatives are obstacles toward one's liberation.
   Enemies are the objects of the perfection of patience.

If you have some static view about your relatives, or if your
relatives or parents have some static view about you and how
you should lead your life to be successful in this world, their
encouragement and their influence is definitely an obstacle
for your spiritual practice. This is how relatives usually are. In
America it seems that parents don't bother their kids and kids
don't bother the parents, at least about life decisions. But in
Tibet, relatives try to influence you to do things that are totally
the opposite of what your spiritual practice is. If someone
encourages you to do spiritual practice, then that person is very
noble, no matter who that person is.

Yet if you don't have relatives, you won't have an easy way
to really improve your patience. There was one guy who was
practicing patience in solitary retreat for six years, and one day
someone came up to him and asked, "What are you practicing?"
He said, "I am practicing patience." The other guy said, "How can
you practice patience when you have no one to be patient with?"
Then the man who'd been practicing said, "How dare you say that
to me! I've been practicing for seven years!" So, to really develop
the quality of patience, you must have an object to practice with.

Pema Jyipa describes the shape of the mountain as like the
shape of Avalokiteshvara's peaceful mudra, and the field itself as
Tara's pure land. There, Pema Jyipa practiced, and many six-
syllable mantras were written. According to Patrul Rinpoche,
wherever he lived was a pure land. There was no difference
between Tara's pure land, which exists in the sambhogakaya
field, and the place where he was living.

It is surrounded by poisonous snakes,
which no devil-minded being would dare cross.
In the foreground, the flowers have blossomed,

227

which are themselves the very manifestation
of Padmasambhava and have appeared to free beings.

The flowers represent Guru Padmasambhava, a manifestation
of Avalokiteshvara.

"At the bottom of the mountain is the beautiful cave-palace
of the noble mother, Tara." Now is the time for the noble
mother to benefit beings. In this generation, there isn't any
deity who can give more blessings than Padmasambhava and
Tara because from the beginning, their motivation has been
concentrated on this degenerate time.

"Even desiring suffering, I experience only happiness."
When you attain realization, there is no way to suffer because
suffering comes from ignorance. When ignorance is completely
conquered by awareness, there is no possibility to suffer, even if
you want to.

"I travel from one happy place to another. A la la! Ultimate
happiness, unchangeable." Ultimate happiness is complete
enlightenment, and that is unchangeable. Until then, there
is some movement and change in one's spiritual realization.
Though the moon doesn't really change, it appears to wax and
wane, from full to slight. In the same way, realization doesn't
change from its nature, but because of purification, it appears
to. The moon can be reflected as many times as there are pools
of water on the ground. That is the benefit.

Conclusion
When Pema Jyipa said these words, they felt very good in
Golden Bee's heart. Golden Bee became a renowned and
excellent practitioner.

In the clear sky of spring blossoms the glorious moon
with its beautiful qualities and silkiness.
Manjushri, you are the innermost wisdom of all the
Victorious Ones.
You are the wisdom in all beings.

To the countless beings who suffer naturally,
Avalokiteshvara, with unblinking eyes,
stretches forth his hand of great compassion.
You are the compassion of all the victorious buddhas
and the love that is inherent in all beings.

Most secret of the secret treasure holders
of the treasures of all the Buddha's teachings,
Vajrapani, you are the activity of all the Victorious Ones
and the naked awareness of all sentient beings.

I pray to the three Bodhisattvas. Bless me.
Inseparable from my guru, you are inseparable
from the crown of my head until liberation.
Take me under your guidance at all times until then.

The Drama of the Flower-Gathering Garden was put down by
Tashi Gelek at the request of others. Peacefully, Shri has done
this work.

Concluding Commentary

Because of our basic intelligence, we can know this is a peach,
this an apple, and this is a table. This basic intelligence is the
seed that Manjushri developed into wisdom. At the end Patrul
Rinpoche is saying that the most victorious is the innermost
wisdom, Manjushri, and the intelligence that we have is also
Manjushri. There is a deity called Manjushri as well.

Bodhisattvas have so much compassion that they don't for a
single minute miss watching carefully, with unblinking eyes, for
how to help sentient beings. Just as we love our children, even
snakes, the angriest beings alive, love their young. That love
and compassion, that natural basic goodness, is the seed that
Avalokiteshvara developed, and it is the compassion of all the
victorious. We also have that seed.

If we really look at our mind, it is insubstantial. This
insubstantial mind is ground openness. That ground openness is

completely naked in its own recognition, and we all have that. All sentient beings have that mind, which turns into Vajrapani, the treasure holder of the Lord Buddha.

Once you motivate yourself to attain enlightenment for the benefit of all sentient beings, from then on, all the buddhas and bodhisattvas throw flowers on you and offer many prayers for you to succeed. From then on, they stay as your crown jewel. Since that is so, Patrul Rinpoche says in this final prayer, "Bless me."

Finally, I'll simply say this about this story. Don't fool yourself, and be consistent in your practice. Always check to see whether what you're doing is right or wrong. Even if you're doing something right, if you're not doing it consistently, there will be no effect. But if you don't fool yourself and you're consistent, then you're a serious practitioner. If you're a serious practitioner, this story is a complete and succinct teaching for you. It is guru, Dharma, and sangha, and there is no need for any other teaching besides this. You can hear other teachings to clarify some of these points, but they're all included in this story.

Acknowledgments

With the publication of *The Bee Story*, Mangala Shri Bhuti introduces a new imprint dedicated solely to the teachings of Dzigar Kongtrul Rinpoche, who named it the *Roar of the Fearless Lion*.

The self-published books from the Roar of the Fearless Lion, and previously Palri Editions, represent the efforts of many people who are involved with the diverse aspects of preserving and spreading Kongtrul Rinpoche's teachings. We would like to extend to all of them our heartfelt gratitude. Our mission is to make selected teachings available to the MSB sangha and the wider public, with the objective of maintaining the highest fidelity to Rinpoche's spoken words and his intention to clearly convey the Dharma to modern readers and listeners.

We also extend a special note of gratitude to Andrew Shakespeare, who provided the inspiration to revisit these first teachings of Rinpoche's to Western students, and to Tara di Gesu, an esteemed artist and thangka painter, who generously provided original illustrations for *The Bee Story*.

EDITING TEAM
Special thanks to Chris Parmentier, who was the main editor of this material. Her skill in working with raw transcripts to clearly bring out the meaning shines through. Her attention to detail has brought these two series of teachings together into this beautifully arranged book.

Other editors who contributed are: Suzy Greanias, Mark Kram, Radha Marcum, Andrew Shakespeare, Markus Stobbs, and Joey Waxman.

PUBLICATION REVIEW
Jennifer Shippee

PRODUCTION LAYOUT
Michael McIlmurray

Dza Patrul Rinpoche

Made in the USA
Las Vegas, NV
15 January 2024

84402284R10134